LINE UPON LINE
PART 2

LINE UPON LINE PART 2

LINE UPON LINE
PART 2

Mrs F. L.Mortimer

Christian Focus Publications

LINE UPON LINE PART 2

ISBN 1-85792-591-2

This edition published in 2000
by
Christian Focus Publications Ltd.
Geanies House, Fearn, Ross-shire,
IV20 1TW, Scotland, Great Britain.
(www.christianfocus.com ~ email:info@christianfocus.com)

Cover design by Owen Daily

Printed and bound in Great Britain
by Cox and Wyman

PREFACE

Mrs Favell Lee Mortimer was born in 1802, the daughter of a London banker. She was religiously educated, and after her conversion at the age of 25, she threw herself with great enthusiasm into benevolent work. In particular, she was responsible for founding some parish schools on her father's estates, and was actively involved in their management.

At the age of 39 the author married Rev Thomas Mortimer, an Episcopal minister, but was widowed nine years later. After his death, she devoted her life to the care of the poor, and to writing books for the young. Her first great success was, "The Peep of Day," which passed through a great number of editions, and was translated into several languages. This was followed by further volumes, which included, "Line upon Line" in two parts. Her books made a lasting impact on the minds of the young in her day, and continue to influence generations long after her death in 1878.

In this edition of "Line Upon Line Part 2", every effort has been made to maintain as much of the original text as possible. It has been edited and adapted out of a desire to make it accessible to the contemporary reader whilst retaining the biblical accuracy and the author's ability to communicate with children.

Particular note should be taken of the new 'Suggestions for Study' which have been added to the start of each section and which include an activity which will involve the child in the next group of devotions.

Our hope is that this volume will be as much of a blessing in teaching today's generation as it was to previous ones.

Family Devotional Guide to the Bible

INTRODUCTION TO THE SERIES

The Family Devotional Guide to the Bible is made up of a series of six books which are excellent tools to use during your family devotional and worship times.

Although each book can be used on its own, the author's original intent was that they be used consecutively so that, starting with The Peep of Day, you and your children can go through the stories from the Bible together and discover the valuable lessons that can be learnt from them.

Using this series, you can progress from the story of Creation right through the Old Testament to the New Testament and the life, death and resurrection of the Lord Jesus Christ, the adventures and lessons of the Apostles and the early Christian Church.

All six books are an excellent family resource.

Family Devotional Guide to the Bible

BOOKS IN THE SERIES

1. The Peep of Day:

Lessons from both Old and New Testaments.

2. Line Upon Line I:

Lessons from Genesis, Exodus, Numbers and Joshua.

3. Line Upon Line II:

Lessons from 1st and 2nd Samuel, 1st and 2nd Kings, Daniel and Ezra.

4. Precept Upon Precept:

Lessons from the New Testament about the life, death and resurrection of Jesus Christ.

5. More About Jesus:

Further lessons from the New Testament about the life, death and resurrection of Jesus Christ.

6. Lines Left Out

Further Old Testament lessons not dealt with in The Peep of Day or Line Upon Line I and II.

USER'S INTRODUCTION

The aim of this book is to lead children to understand and to delight in the Scriptures.

If adults can meet with difficulties in the biblical text which commentaries will help them to overcome, children will obviously come across many more, some of which this book may help to clear up. Obviously the direction and teaching of a loving parent is the greatest help any child can have in understanding the Bible and its teaching, but this book and others in the series, will re-inforce that teaching and where parental guidance is not available this book will in some way help to fill that gap.

You should take particular note of the newly created 'Suggestions for Study' which have been added to the start of each section and which include an activity to involve your child in the next group of devotions.

Each chapter also contains a memory verse that relates in some way to the content of the chapter. Use these to encourage your child to commit these verses to memory as part of your study of the Bible.

In addition you will notice small numbers contained in the text of the chapters. These relate to notes provided at the end of each lesson, which you can use to encourage your child to get to know their way round their Bible by finding and reading the passages listed.

CONTENTS

LINE UPON LINE PART 2

SECTION 3: 1 & 2 KINGS

SECTION 4: DANIEL

SECTION 5: EZRA

SECTION 1

1 SAMUEL

Introduction

After settling in the Promised Land, the Israelites were led by Judges – people chosen by God to lead them in times of need. In 1 Samuel, we learn that the people call upon Samuel, the last of these Judges, to tell God that they want a King. Samuel believes that this amounts to a turning away from God and warns them that this decision will in the future bring suffering upon them.

The first King of the Israelites, chosen by God, is a man named Saul. At first, he is a good king, who follows God's ways. However, as we read on, we find out about his gradual disobedience and jealousy towards David (who will be his successor). And so, we begin to see why God had warned the people about wanting a King.

Some Suggestions for Study

Before each chapter in this section, think of some leaders of people that you know about. They may be historical leaders, or some of today's kings, queens, presidents, prime ministers, captains or generals. They might be a leader in your town, school, church or youth group. Maybe you could get a history book or newspaper and see what you can learn about them. Think about how they became leaders – were they chosen by people? Did they force their way to power through strength? Are they or were they good leaders or bad? Pray for the leaders who affect your life, that God would guide their lives.

CHAPTER 1
SAMUEL AND THE PIOUS MOTHER

1 Sam. 1; 2:1-11.

You have heard how the Israelites came into the land of Canaan. I shall now tell you what happened to them in Canaan after Joshua died.

Do you remember that the tabernacle was placed in Shiloh? The high priest lived in Shiloh, that he might offer sacrifices in the tabernacle. I am now going to tell you of a high priest called Eli. Eli was a very good old man.

A great many people used to come up every year to Shiloh to worship God at the tabernacle. Among the people who came up to worship there was a man who had two wives. You know that people might have two wives a long while ago, though they may not have two now.

One of these wives was a very good woman and she was called Hannah, but she had no child. The other wife had a great many children. She was unkind and laughed at Hannah. She said that God gave Hannah no child because He did not love her. This was not true, for God loved Hannah very much. Poor Hannah used to cry sometimes when the other wife spoke so unkindly to her.

Once, when Hannah had come to Shiloh and the other wife had been laughing at her, poor Hannah went to the tabernacle to pray to God. Eli was in the court of the tabernacle. He was sitting upon a high seat and he saw Hannah come into the court. Now poor Hannah was praying to God in a very low voice and her eyes were red with weeping. When Eli saw Hannah he thought she had been drinking too much wine and he spoke roughly to her and said, "Why do you drink so much?" How ashamed poor Hannah must have been when Eli said this to her before all the people! But she answered him very meekly and said, "I have not been drinking; I have been praying to God, for I am very unhappy."

When Eli heard this, he spoke kindly to her and said, "May God give you what you have been asking for."

What had poor Hannah been praying for? She had prayed for a little child and she had promised God that she would bring the child up to serve Him and teach people about Him.

Hannah was glad when Eli spoke so kindly to her and she wiped away her tears and went home, looking quite happy. You see it is a good thing to pray to the Lord when we are unhappy. I hope you do so, when you are sick, or when you are in disgrace, or when people are unkind to you.

Hannah went away from Shiloh to the place where she lived in Canaan and God sent her a little baby and she called his name "Samuel."

When Samuel was a baby, Hannah did not go up to Shiloh, but when he was a little child of about three years old, she took him up to Shiloh with her.[1]

Hannah did not forget her promise to bring up her child to teach people about God; Hannah did not mean to keep him always at home with her, though she loved him very much; for she wished the good old high priest Eli to bring him up and to teach him. So she brought the child to Eli and said to him, "I am the woman that you once saw in the court of the tabernacle, praying to God; I was praying for this child and God has heard my prayer so I wish the child to be brought up to serve God."

Eli took the little boy to live with him. Hannah sang a beautiful song of praise to God for his goodness in hearing her prayers and then she left her dear little Samuel and went home again with her husband.

Do you think she ever came to see her child? Yes, every

year and she always brought him a present of a coat such as the people wore in those days.

It was a linen coat down to his feet and it had long sleeves. Samuel also used to wear a linen decorated apron, like the priests, though Samuel was not a priest himself. God had put His Spirit into Samuel's heart, so that he liked serving the Lord in the tabernacle and seeing the sacrifices offered and hearing the Lord praised by the priests and the people. As he grew older he pleased God more and more and a great many people loved him. How glad Hannah must have been when she came to see him to hear that he was a good child! It makes your parents very happy to hear that you are good. And the angels are pleased when you are good and Jesus your Saviour is pleased. I hope you will be like little Samuel and be God's children while you are very young.

Questions for Chapter 1

Why did people come up to Shiloh?
Who was Eli?
Why was Hannah very unhappy?
Why did Eli speak roughly to her?
What was Hannah praying for when Eli spoke unkindly to her?
Why did Hannah bring Samuel to Eli?
Why was Samuel so good a child?

Scripture Verses

Trusting God's guidance for our lives.

'Trust in the Lord with all thine heart and lean not unto thine own understanding. In all thy ways acknowledge him and he shall direct thy paths.' - (Prov 3:5,6).

Notes to Chapter 1

[1] As the priests began to learn the work of the sanctuary at three years of age, it is probable that Samuel (though only a Levite, 1 Chron. 6:16-28), began to be taught at that age. - (2 Chronicles 31:16).

* * * * * * * * * *

CHAPTER 2
SAMUEL AND THE LITTLE PROPHET

1 Sam. 2: 12, and 23 to end.

You have heard how Samuel lived with old Eli at Shiloh.

He did not live in the tabernacle, but in some tents very near it.[1]

You would like to know whether Eli had any children of his own. He had two sons, who were grown-up men and they were priests who offered sacrifices at the altar.

I suppose you think that Eli's sons were good, because Eli was good; but I am sorry to tell you that they were very wicked men. They did not love God, they only cared for eating and amusing themselves and they did not wish to please God. Eli was good himself, but he did not punish his wicked sons and that was very wrong of Eli. Do your parents punish you when you are bad-tempered or are disobedient or tell lies? They punish you to make you good.

Eli heard of the wicked things that his sons did and he said to them, "Why do you do such wicked things? Everybody tells me of your wickedness. Oh, my sons, the Lord will be angry with you and punish you." But Eli's sons paid no attention to what their father said and went on with their bad ways.

At last a good man came to Eli and told him that God was very angry and that He would let both his sons be killed in one day.

It must have grieved Eli to hear this. God was displeased

with Eli for not having punished his sons. Yet Eli was a good man and God loved him.

The two sons went on in their wickedness. And now you shall hear something else that God said.

One evening old Eli was lying in bed and little Samuel was lying in another bed a little way off. Samuel heard a voice calling him, "Samuel." Samuel thought that Eli had called him and he answered, "Here am I";[2] and then he got out of bed and ran to Eli, to know what he wanted. You see what a kind little child Samuel was and how ready he was to wait upon Eli.

But Eli said to Samuel, "I did not call you"; then Samuel went and lay down again.

Soon afterwards Samuel heard someone call him again, "Samuel." So he went again to Eli and said, "Here am I, for you did call me." But Eli said, "I did not call, my son; lie down again."

Then Samuel lay down and he soon heard the voice again saying, "Samuel." Then he felt sure that it was Eli who called him and he went to him and said, "Here am I, for you did call me."

Now Eli knew who it was who had called Samuel.

Do you know who it was? It was the Lord.

So Eli told Samuel to lie down again and when he heard the voice, to answer, "Speak, Lord, for your servant is listening." Samuel was to call himself God's servant.

So Samuel went and lay down again and soon the Lord came and stood by him and called as before, "Samuel, Samuel." Then Samuel answered, "Speak, Lord, for your servant is listening." God had never spoken to Samuel before. Samuel must have longed to know what the Lord had to say to him. It was something very sad and dreadful; it was about Eli.

God told Samuel that He would soon punish Eli's sons for

their wickedness and that He was displeased with Eli for not having punished them.

After God had finished speaking, Samuel remained in his bed and Eli did not call him. Samuel did not like to tell Eli that God was displeased with him.

So when the morning came, Samuel did not go to Eli, but began to open the doors round about the tabernacle; for it was Samuel's job to open the doors. Soon Eli called Samuel; for he wanted to know what God had said to Samuel. Eli begged Samuel to tell everything to him and to hide nothing from him.

Then little Samuel told Eli all that God had said.

How grieved Eli must have been when he heard that God would punish his sons and that He was displeased with him; but Eli answered very meekly and said, "Let the Lord do what he pleases." Eli really loved God, though he had done one wrong thing.

After this God often spoke to Samuel and told him how He would punish wicked people. Samuel used to tell people what God had said and all that he told them came true. Samuel was a prophet; a prophet is a person to whom the Lord tells what He means to make happen.

People paid great attention to what Samuel said, but still many people went on doing wicked things. The people in Shiloh were very wicked and God determined soon to punish them as well as Eli's sons. But God loved Samuel. What a happy child Samuel was!

If you love God, I am sure that He loves you; for He has said, "I love them that love me." Pray to God to make you love Him a great deal more and to make you good, like Samuel. I hope that you will never be like Eli's wicked sons.

Questions for Chapter 2

Were Eli's sons good or bad?
Why was God displeased with Eli?
What did God say would happen to Eli's sons?
When did God first speak to Samuel?
What did Eli tell Samuel to say to God when he spoke to Him?
What did God tell Samuel when He spoke to him?
How did Eli behave, when Samuel told him what the Lord had said?
What is a prophet?
Was Samuel a prophet?

Scripture Verses

An encouragement to love God.

'Oh, love the Lord, all ye his saints: for the Lord preserveth the faithful and plentifully rewardeth the proud doer.' - (Ps. 31:23).

Notes for Chapter 2

1. 2 Chronicles 31:2. 2. 1 Samuel 3:4

* * * * * * * * * *

CHAPTER 3
SAMUEL AND THE ARK IN THE BATTLE

1 Sam. 4:1-18.

I shall tell you today how God punished Eli's sons; but first I must speak to you about some people who lived in the land of Canaan, called the Philistines.

The Philistines lived in some of the towns of Canaan; they were wicked people who worshipped idols and they hated the Israelites; they often fought against the Israelites and took away their things. When God was pleased with the Israelites, He did not let the Philistines hurt them, but now He was angry with the Israelites.

One day a great number of Philistines came out of their towns to fight against the Israelites. They brought some tents with them and slept in them at night. The Israelites heard that the Philistines were coming to fight against them; so a great number of Israelites took their swords and spears and placed their tents near the tents of the Philistines. In the morning the Philistines and the Israelites fought with each other. Who do you think conquered? The Philistines. Yes; God did not help the Israelites as He used to do, so the Israelites were frightened and ran back into their tents.

Now the Israelites ought to have prayed to God to forgive their sins; but instead of praying they said, "Let us send for the ark of God. If the ark were here, we would be able to conquer the Philistines."

You remember that the ark was a golden box, on which God sometimes sat in a cloud. But would the ark save them? No, only God can save people.

The Israelites sent a person to Shiloh to instruct the priests to being the ark to the tents. The sons of Eli, you know, were priests. The brought the ark to the tents of the Israelites. When the Israelites saw the ark, they were delighted and they gave a very loud shout to show their joy. The shout could be heard a great way off. The Philistines heard the shout and they asked why the Israelites shouted. Soon they heard that the ark of the God of Israel had come to the tents of the Israelites. Then the Philistines were afraid and they said, "If the God of the Israelites would help them, what would we do? For their God once killed Pharaoh and all his men and He could kill us too. Oh, let us be very brave and let us fight with all our strength."

So the Philistines and the Israelites came out of their tents to fight and the priests brought the ark on their shoulders.

But God did not help the Israelites. They were soon afraid and ran back to their tents and a great many of them were killed and the two sons of Eli were killed, as God had said.

What became of the ark of God? The Philistines took it. How pleased they were to get the ark! They carried it back to the towns where they lived.

Eli had not come to the battle. He had stayed in Shiloh; he was very unhappy about the ark. He wanted to know what had become of it, so he sat upon a high seat just at the gate of Shiloh.

At last a man came running along the road; he had been fighting in the battle and he came to tell the people in Shiloh all that had happened. He had put dust upon his head and he had torn his clothes to show that he had sad news to tell; for people used to put dust on their heads and to tear their clothes, when they were unhappy. But Eli was very old and he was blind and did not see the man and did not know that the man had sad news to tell. When the man told the people in Shiloh what had happened, the people cried out very loud with grief and Eli heard them crying and asked why they cried and the man answered, "I am just come from the place where the Israelites were fighting." Then Eli said, "What has happened there?" Then the man said, "The Israelites have run away from the Philistines and a great many Israelites have been killed and your two sons are dead and the ark of God is taken."

When Eli heard that the ark was taken, he was very unhappy indeed; he was sitting on a high seat that had no back and he fell backwards and broke his neck; for he was a very old man and very heavy. He was almost a hundred years old.

What a very sad way of dying this was, instead of dying in his bed? How grieved Samuel must have been when he heard how Eli had died! Where did Eli's soul go? To heaven. Eli loved God very much.

Why was Eli so sorry that the ark was taken? Because the ark was the throne where God used to sit and he did not like wicked people to have it; so you see that Eli loved God very much.

Where were the souls of Eli's sons gone? I know they were gone into darkness; for God had said that He would not forgive them.[1] But God forgave Eli all his sins, though He punished him before he died.

You will like to hear what the Philistines did with the ark of God. I will tell you about it next time.

Questions for Chapter 3

Where did the Philistines live?
Why did God once let the Philistines hurt the Israelites?
Why did the Israelites send for the ark?
Who brought the ark? What became of the ark?
What happened to Eli's sons?
What news grieved Eli so much that he fell backwards?
Why was Eli so grieved at hearing the ark was taken?
Did God love Eli? Why did God punish him?
Did God forgive him?

Scripture Verse

God corrects his children because he loves them.
'For whom the Lord loveth he chasteneth and scourgeth every son whom he receiveth.' - (Heb. 12:6).

Notes for Chapter 3

1. 1 Samuel 3:14.

CHAPTER 4
SAMUEL AND THE GOD DAGON

1 Sam. 5; 6; 7:4.

Do you now wish to know what the Philistines did with the ark?

They were delighted at getting the ark of the God of Israel; for they knew that He was a very great God. The Philistines took the ark to one of their cities, or towns and they put it in the house of their idol. Their idol's name was Dagon. The Philistines had made an image like a man and they called it Dagon and they had built a house for Dagon and they had set Dagon up on a high place; so they used to come and worship Dagon very often in this house.

The Philistines left the ark all night in the house of Dagon; the next morning they got up early and went into the idol's house. But what do you think they saw when they went in?

They saw that their idol had fallen down from the high place and was lying upon his face before the ark.

Who had thrown Dagon down? It was God, who wished to show the Philistines that He was stronger than idols and that He hated idols.

The Philistines were not quite sure that it was God who had thrown Dagon on the ground; so they lifted up their idol and set him in his place again near the ark and then left him.

The next morning they rose up early and came into the idol's house. What do you think they saw this time?

Dagon had fallen down again upon his face before the ark and this time Dagon was broken; his head and his hands were broken off from his body. The Philistines were very sorry their idol was broken. I do not know whether they mended the idol or whether they set him up again, but God soon made something much worse happen to the Philistines. God made them very ill indeed and full of pain. They said one to another, "What shall we do with the ark? For it shall not stay in this city any longer." So they sent it to another city, where some other Philistines lived. What do you think happened to the people of that city, when the ark of God came into it?

They fell very ill indeed and a great many of them died. So the people of the city sent it to another city of the Philistines. The people of the other city were very frightened when they saw the ark coming; they said, "We shall die now the ark is brought here."

Soon they fell very ill and a great many of the people died and the city was full of people groaning and crying.

At last the Philistines thought they would send the ark back to the Israelites; but they did not feel quite sure that the God of Israel had been angry with them for keeping the ark.

Had the God of Israel been angry with them? Yes, you know that it was God who made them so ill and who had killed so many of them.

The Philistines made a plan for sending back the ark. This was their plan. They said, "We will put the ark in a cart and we will take two cows that have never drawn a cart before and we will tie them to the cart and we will shut up their calves in this place where we live. No one shall drive the cows, but we will see what they will do. If the God of Israel be so great, He can make the cows take the ark back to the Israelites. If the cows leave their calves and go to the place where the Israelites live, then we shall be quite sure that it was the God of Israel who made us so ill, to punish us for keeping the ark."

This was the plan of the Philistines. They had heard how God once sent plagues to Pharaoh and they were afraid in case God would do the same to them. They said, "We will not harden our hearts, as Pharaoh and the people of Egypt did."

The Philistines took two cows that gave milk and tied them to a cart and shut up their calves at home and they laid the ark of God upon the cart and they watched to see what the cows would do.

Then God made the cows do a wonderful thing. They drew the cart, without being driven, along the road which led to the place where the Israelites lived. They lowed as they went and never once turned out of the road.

Some of the Philistines followed the cart.

At last the cart came to a place where some of the Israelites were reaping corn in a field. These Israelites looked up and saw the cart coming and soon they saw the ark and they were very glad indeed. The cows brought the cart into the field and then stopped by the side of a great stone.

Questions for Chapter 4

Where did the Philistines first place the ark?
What happened to Dagon?
What other punishment did God send to the Philistines for keeping the ark?
Why did the Philistines at last determine to send it back to the Israelites?
Who carried it back?
Where had the Philistines shut up the calves of the cows?
Why had they shut them up at home?
Where did the cows stop?

Scripture Verse

God does not tolerate the worship of false gods.

'I am the Lord: that is my name: and my glory will I not give to another, neither my praise to graven images.' - (Isa. 42:8).

CHAPTER 5
SAMUEL AND THE DISOBEDIENT LOOK

1 Sam. 6:13; 7:1 to end.

The Israelites in the field took the ark out of the cart and placed it on the great stone and they took the cart and cut it up for wood for a sacrifice and they killed the two cows and burned them as a sacrifice. They did this to show they were grateful to God who had made the cows bring the ark back.

The Philistines were surprised at the wonderful thing that God had done and they went back to their own land. Ought they not to have left off worshipping idols, when they saw how great the God of Israel was? Yes, they should have burned their idols when they got home and only worshipped the true God. But they did go on worshipping idols and God was angry with them for it.

And the Israelites did a thing that displeased God very much. They looked into the ark.[1] You know what there was inside the ark. The book of stone on which the ten commandments were written.

God is very angry when people dare to disobey Him; so He made those Israelites fall very ill and a great many of them died. Then they were afraid of keeping the ark in their city and they sent messages to some other Israelites to come and fetch it and they came and fetched it and put it in the house of a man. This man lived upon a hill and he and his son took care of the ark in one of the rooms of his house.

Do you know why the ark was not sent back to the tabernacle at Shiloh? The people of Shiloh had worshipped idols and so God was angry and would not let the ark go back to Shiloh.[2]

It was very kind of God to let the ark come again into the place where the Israelites lived.

Questions for Chapter 5

What did the Israelites sacrifice to God, to thank Him for letting the ark come back?
Did the Philistines go on worshipping idols after the wonderful thing that God had done?
How did some of the Israelites offend God after the ark was brought back?
Who alone might look in?
Was the ark taken back to Shiloh?
Why not?
Where was it kept?

Scripture Verse

People turn from God to idolatry.

'Professing themselves to be wise, they became fools, And changed the glory of the uncorruptible God into an image made like to corruptible man and to birds and fourfooted beasts and creeping things.' - (Rom. 1:22,23).

Notes for Chapter 5

1. Num. 4:20; This ban (addressed to the Levites) applied to all except the priests.
2. Ps. 78:58,60.

CHAPTER 6
SAMUEL AND THE UNGRATEFUL WISH

1 Sam. 8

Who was the king of the Israelites? God was the King of the Israelites. When Samuel was grown up to be a man, he was called a judge; but he was not a king. He used to tell the people what God wished them to do and he used to punish bad people. Moses had once been the judge of Israel and Joshua had once been the judge and Eli had once been the judge. Now Samuel was called the judge. He did not sit on a throne, or wear a crown, as kings do and he always asked God to tell him what the people ought to do and then he told the people what God had said. The Israelites ought to have been very glad that God was their King. No other king was so good and so great as He was.

You will be sorry to hear that at last they grew tired of having God for their king. They said, "We would like to have a king that would go out to battle before us." They wanted to have a king that they could see. So they came to Samuel and said, "Give us a king."

Samuel was very sorry to hear this and he went and prayed to the Lord. Do you think that God would let the Israelites have a king? Yes, He would; He was displeased with them for wishing for a king, but as they wanted a king, God said they would have one.

So Samuel called the Israelites together to speak to them and then he said, "God will let you have a king, but this is the way in which the king will treat you.

"He will make your sons work for him; some of them will

run before his chariots and some will make swords and spears for him and some will plough his ground and reap his corn and some of your daughters will bake and cook and make nice things for him to eat and he will take away many of your fields and gardens and corn and sheep from you and give them to whom he pleases and then you will be sorry that you wished for a king and you will cry to God and He will not hear you."

Did the Israelites still wish for a king? Yes; they would not listen to what Samuel said; but they cried out, "We will have a king."

Then all the people went home.

Who do you think would say which man was to be a king?

God was to choose the king and God would tell Samuel who was to be king.

I shall tell you in the next story about the man whom God chose to be the king of Israel.

Questions for Chapter 6

Was Samuel the king of Israel, or was he the judge?
Who was the king of Israel?
Why was it wicked in the Israelites to wish for a king?
Why did they wish for a king?
How did Samuel say their king would treat them?
Did the Israelites still wish for a king?
Who would choose a king for them?

Scripture Verse

The Lord is ultimately King over all.
The Lord *is* King forever and ever...' - (Ps. 10:16)

CHAPTER 7
SAUL AND THE KING

1 Sam. 9; 10:1; 17 to end.

There was a young man whose father had some fields and sheep and cows and donkeys. One day three donkeys were lost; so the young man went to look for them among the hills and fields. The young man's name was Saul. He took a servant with him and he looked for the donkeys a long while, but he could not find them. At last Saul came near the city where Samuel lived.

The servant said to Saul, "I have heard that there is a man in that city who is a prophet; all he says comes true. Let us ask him where the donkeys are." Then Saul said to his servant, "Come, let us go." So Saul and the servant went into the city and as they went along they met Samuel.[1] Saul and the servant had never seen Samuel before, so they did not know who he was. By now Samuel was an old man, his hair was long[2] and he used to wear a cloak.

Saul spoke to this old man and said, "Can you tell me where the prophet's house is?"

Samuel answered, "I am the prophet."

Did Samuel know who Saul was? Yes, he did; for though Samuel had never seen him before, God had told Samuel that he would meet a man just at that time, who was to be the king of Israel. Samuel knew who Saul was and he knew that Saul wanted to ask him where the donkeys were.

Before Saul had told him that he had lost some donkeys, Samuel said, "The donkeys that you lost three days ago are found." And Samuel told Saul that he had a great deal to say to him and that he must come home with him that evening and that he would let him go away the next morning.

So Saul and the servant went to Samuel's house and Samuel took Saul to the top of his house and talked to him alone; but I do not know what he said to him.

The next morning they all got up very early, as soon as it was light and Samuel walked with Saul and the servant through the city. When they came to the outside of the city, Samuel said to Saul, "Bid the servant pass on before." So the servant passed on before and Samuel and Saul stood still together quite alone.

Then Samuel took a bottle of oil, that he had brought with him and poured it on Saul's head and said to him, "God has chosen you to be king over Israel."

Why did Samuel pour the oil upon Saul's head? It was as a sign that he was to be the king. Pouring oil upon a person is called "anointing."

After Samuel had anointed Saul, they parted from each other. Saul went on his way and returned to his friends; but he did not tell anyone that he was to be king of Israel.

Soon afterwards Samuel called all the Israelites together, to tell them who was to be the king.

Samuel first told them it was very wicked not to like to have God for their king and then he showed them the man who was to be the king. When the people saw Saul they were very pleased, for he was taller than any of the Israelites; no one else reached higher than his shoulder. The Israelites wished to have a king that would look very grand when he went out to battle.

The Israelites shouted when they saw him and cried out, "God save the king!"

When the people had seen their king they went home to their houses.

You will soon hear what sort of a king Saul was, whether he loved God, or whether he did not.

Did the Israelites deserve to have a good king? No. How ungratefully they had behaved to God, who had been so kind to them! How ungrateful they were to Samuel who had been their judge! But Samuel was not angry with them, he was only sorry that they were wicked.

Questions for Chapter 7

What was Saul looking for when he first came to Samuel?
What did he ask Saul?
Did Samuel know that Saul was coming?
Where did Saul spend the night?
What did Samuel do to Saul next morning?
What was pouring oil on a person's head, to make him king, called?
Why were the Israelites pleased when they saw Saul?
What did they cry out?

Scripture Verse

Samuel warned the people about wanting a man as King rather than trusting God.

And ye shall cry out in that day because of your king which ye shall have chosen you and the Lord will not hear you in that day.' - (1 Sam. 8:18).

Notes for Chapter 7

1. The history of the sacrifice is omitted because it would not be well understood, without the knowledge of many complicated details, unknown to the young pupil.

2. Samuel was a Nazarite and wore long hair - (See 1 Sam. 1:11; compare with Num. 6).

CHAPTER 8
SAUL AND THE DISOBEDIENT DEED

1 Sam. 15

I have told you how God made Saul the king of Israel. Saul sat upon a throne and wore a crown and went to battle in a chariot. He was a brave man and could fight well against wicked soldiers who tried to hurt the Israelites.

Samuel used often to come and see him and advise him to serve God. Samuel wished Saul to be good and he often prayed for him.

At last God chose to see whether Saul would do all He commanded him to do. You remember how God once tried Abraham and how Abraham did what God commanded him, because he loved God. What was Saul to do?

There were some wicked people, who lived near the land of Canaan, called the Am-al-ek-ites. God was very angry with them and He chose that they would all be killed.

One day Samuel came to Saul and said to him, "God desires you to go and fight against the Amalekites and kill them all - men, women and children and oxen and sheep and camels and donkeys."

Saul got a great army of Israelites and went to the Amalekites and he conquered them. Then Saul commanded his soldiers to kill them with their swords, as God had told him. But he thought he would like to take the king of the Amalekites back to Canaan with him, so he would not let him be killed. I think Saul liked to bring the king home with him, because he thought it was a grand and fine thing to have a king shut up near him in Canaan. Neither did Saul kill the fat and strong oxen and sheep; he only killed those that were thin and weak. Saul wished to be rich and to have a many cattle.

Did Saul obey God? No, Saul did not love God; so Saul did not wish to obey Him. If you love God you will like to obey Him.

That night God spoke to Samuel and told him that He was very angry with Saul. Samuel was grieved to hear this and he prayed to God the rest of the night.

Questions for Chapter 8

How did God try Saul to see whether he loved Him?
Did Saul destroy the Amalekites?
What did Saul bring home?
Did he kill all the cattle? Why not?
How was it Samuel knew what Saul had done?

Scripture Verse

What God truly seeks in somebody.
'And Samuel said, Hath the Lord as great delight in burnt offerings and sacrifices, as in obeying the voice of the Lord? Behold, to obey is better than sacrifice and to hearken than the fat of rams.' - (1 Sam. 15:22).

* * * * * * * * * *

CHAPTER 9
SAUL AND THE PUNISHMENT

The next morning Samuel went to look for Saul, for God had told him many things that he must say to him.

Saul did not know that Samuel knew of his wickedness; so he tried to make Samuel think that he had done all that God had told him.

When Saul saw Samuel, he pretended to be glad to see him

and said, "I have done the commandment of the Lord." Then Samuel said, "What then is this bleating of sheep and lowing of oxen that I hear?"

Now Saul saw that Samuel knew what he had done. He saw it would be of no use to say that he had not saved the sheep and oxen, so he began to make excuses for himself.

Saul said, "It was the people who would not kill the fat sheep and oxen."

Was it the people who had saved the sheep and oxen? Had not Saul saved them too? And why did Saul let the people do wickedly? Was he not the king? Should he not have made them do what was right?

Would God like those sheep and oxen to be offered in sacrifice to Him? No, God would rather that Saul would obey Him than that he would offer sacrifices.

Then Samuel told Saul that God was very angry with him and did not mean to let him be king much longer.

Saul was very frightened when he heard that God would punish him and he said to Samuel, "Do stay and pray to God with me." But Saul was not really sorry; he was only afraid of being punished. Samuel knew that he was not sorry for having offended God, who had been so good to him, so Samuel would not stay with Saul. Then Saul took hold of Samuel's cloak, to hinder him from going away and he tore the cloak.

Samuel stopped and said to Saul, "God has torn the land of Canaan from you and He has given it to a man that is better than you are. God has done it already and He will not change His mind."

Saul begged Samuel very much to stay with him and to pray to God with him, that the people might not know that God was angry with him. You see that Saul cared more about what people thought of him, than about God being pleased with him.

At last Samuel said that he would worship God with him.

Then Samuel wanted to see the king of the Amalekites, whom Saul had saved alive.

This king was a very wicked, cruel man and God chose that he would be killed. He had hoped that, as Saul had not killed him, he would not die; but Samuel took a sword and killed him.

Then Samuel left Saul and he never came to see him any more; but he still was very sorry to think that he was so wicked.

I hope that when you offend God you will feel sorry. If you love God, you will not like to grieve Him. Saul did not love God; he only cared about being punished.

Do you know whom God intended to be king instead of Saul? I will soon tell you his name. He will be a better man than Saul.

Why was it so wicked of Saul not to kill the king of the Amalekites and the fat cattle? Because God had told him to kill them. We ought to do what God tells us to do. Has He told *you* to kill wicked people? No, but He has told you to pray to Him and to be kind and to speak the truth and, first of all, to believe on the Lord Jesus Christ.

Questions for Chapter 9

What excuse did Saul make for himself?

What punishment did Samuel tell Saul that God would give him?

Why did Saul wish Samuel to pray with him?

Why was Saul not sorry for having offended God?

Who killed the king of the Amalekites?

Has God told you to kil? What has God told you to do?[1]

Scripture Verse

Better to fear God rather than people.
'The fear of man bringeth a snare: but whoso putteth his trust in the Lord shall be safe.' - (Prov. 29:25)

Notes for Chapter 9

1. It is a good exercise for children to be asked to list the things they ought to do. This kind of listing is very interesting to children and teaches them to their own daily actions.

* * * * * * * * * *

CHAPTER 10
DAVID AND THE YOUNG SHEPHERD

1 Sam. 16:1-15.

Samuel did not know whom God meant to be king instead of Saul. At last God said to him, "Fill a horn with oil and go to Jesse, who lives in Bethlehem, for I have chosen one of his sons as the king."

Jesse was an old man and he had a great many sons who were grown up. Samuel found Jesse and his sons in Bethlehem. Then Samuel looked at the eldest of Jesse's sons, to see whether he was the man that God had chosen to be king.

Now this son was a very tall, fine-looking man, who seemed fit to be king and Samuel thought to himself, "Surely this is the one that God will choose to anoint."

But God told Samuel that He had not chosen him. God does not care how a person looks, but God cares for the heart. Now the heart of Jesse's eldest son did not please God and this time God was going to choose a king who loved Him in his heart.

Then Samuel looked at Jesse's second son; but when he saw him he said that God had not chosen him. Then Samuel looked at the third son; but God had not chosen him. Then he looked at the fourth; neither had God chosen him. Then Samuel looked at the fifth, next at the sixth and last of all at the seventh and yet God had not chosen any of them.

So Samuel said to Jesse, "Have you any more children?"

And Jesse answered, "I have one more child, the youngest and he is looking after the sheep." Then Samuel said, "Send and fctch him; I want to see him immediately."

So Jesse sent a person to ask this youngest son to come to him.

The name of this son was David. He was not a grown-up man, but only a boy. He had a beautiful colour on his cheeks and his eyes had a pleasant look.

But did he love God in his heart? Yes; he did love God.

When he came in, God said to Samuel, "Arise and anoint him; for this is he." So Samuel took the horn of oil and anointed him, while his seven brothers stood by. Then Samuel went back to his own house.

You will hear a great deal about David. God did not mean him to be king yet; but David knew that he certainly would be king one day. He went on keeping his father's sheep. As he watched them, he played on his harp and sang sweet songs of praise to God. His songs are called "Psalms."

Do you think that David wished to be king? I do not think he wanted to sit on a throne and to wear a crown, but I know that he would like to call people together to praise God. When David was king, he could have people taught about God and he could be kind to poor people and he could punish wicked people.

When Samuel poured the oil on David's head, God made His Spirit come on him, to make him very wise and brave and fit to be a king; for it is God who makes people wise and brave.

Questions for Chapter 10

Why did God command Samuel to go to Bethlehem?
Why did Samuel not anoint Jesse's eldest son?
How many sons had Jesse?
Where was David when Jesse sent for him?
What did Samuel do to David?
What were the songs called that David used to sing?

Scripture Verse

King David a leader who followed God's will.
'And when he had removed him, he raised up unto them David to be their king; to whom also he gave testimony and said, I have found David the son of Jesse, a man after mine own heart, which shall fulfil all my will.' - (Acts 13:22).

* * * * * * * * * *

CHAPTER 11
DAVID AND THE HARP

1 Sam. 16:14 to end.

Did Saul know who was to be king instead of him? No, Samuel did not tell Saul what he had done. Saul would have been very angry if he had known that David had been anointed but he did not know it.

Yet Saul was very unhappy. God had let a wicked spirit come into him. Saul felt frightened and uneasy, so that he could not rest. He lived in a fine house called a palace, but this did not make him happy; he had many servants to wait upon him, but they could do him no good. You see what a sad thing it is to offend God. God can make people happy and He can make them unhappy.

What should Saul have done, now he was so unhappy? He

should have prayed to God to forgive him. But he did not love praying to God.

Saul's servants saw that he had a wicked spirit in him and they said to him, "Shall we look for a man who can play very sweetly on the harp? Perhaps, if you were to listen to very sweet music, you might get well."

Then Saul answered his servants, "Look for such a man and bring him to me."

Whom could the servants send for? One of them had heard of David and he said to Saul, "I have seen one of the sons of Jesse, who lives at Bethlehem and he can play beautifully on the harp. Besides this he is a very brave young man, who can fight well. He can speak very wisely and he is very handsome and God loves him. Shall I send for him?"

Saul said that he would have this young man sent for. Some of Saul's servants sent to Jesse and said, "King Saul wishes to see your son David, who takes care of the sheep."

Jesse said that David might go and he instructed David to take a present to king Saul. What was the present? Some bread, a kid (which is a young goat) and a bottle of wine. David put all these things upon a donkey and brought them to Saul. When Saul saw David, he loved him very much. Perhaps Saul loved him because he had a sweet look and could play well on the harp; but God loved him because he wished to please Him.

Saul liked David so much that he wished David to stay with him for a long time and to be always near him. So Saul sent a message to Jesse to say that he wished to keep him.

David very often played to Saul upon the harp and when David played, Saul grew better and at last grew quite well.

At last David left Saul and fed his father's sheep as he used to do.

I think David liked taking care of the sheep better than living with Saul; for Saul was wicked and many of his servants were wicked.

David was very happy when he was alone, thinking about God. Did you ever hear any of David's psalms? In one of these psalms he calls God his shepherd. David took great care of his sheep and led them to places where green fresh grass grew and to smooth and clear water and he made them lie down on the softest grass, in cool places by the river's side. While David was taking so much care of his sheep, he thought that God took still more care of him and he said, "The Lord is my shepherd, I shall not want. He makes me lie down in green pastures and beside the still waters." What are pastures? Grass. And what are still waters? Smooth waters.

Have you a shepherd? I hope that the Lord is your Shepherd, too and that you are His dear lambs. Jesus is the Good Shepherd, who died to save you. He loves you very much and wishes to make you happy. Do you wish to be His lambs? Jesus will be so kind to you. He will keep you from Satan and He will put His Spirit in you. He will comfort you when you are unhappy and at last He will take you to heaven. How happy are those children who love Jesus!

Questions for Chapter 11

Did Saul know who was to be king instead of him?
What came into Saul?
What did Saul's servants advise him to do to make him well?
Where did David go when Saul was well?
Do you remember any of the psalms of David?
What are psalms? What are still waters?
What has your Shepherd done for you?

Scripture Verse

Jesus, our source of comfort and help.
'Come unto me, all ye that labour and are heavy laden and I will give you rest.' - (Matt. 11:28).

* * * * * * * * * *

CHAPTER 12
DAVID AND THE GIANT GOLIATH

1 Sam. 17:1-37.

You remember who the Philistines were. They were wicked people, who lived in some of the cities of Canaan. The Israelites often fought against the Philistines.

One day a great number of Philistines came and placed their tents on the top of a hill in Canaan. When Saul heard it he came with a great number of Israelites and they placed their tents on another hill. The Philistines and the Israelites could see each other in their tents and they intended to fight against each other; but they did not choose to fight immediately.

There was one man among the Philistines whose name was Goliath. He was called a giant, because he was very tall indeed. He was ten feet high.[1] He was very strong and big and he could fight well. He wore armour. What is armour? Clothes made of iron and bronze; people used to wear armour so that arrows and swords and spears might not hurt them easily.

He wore a bronze helmet upon his head and he wore a coat of iron; his legs were covered with bronze. He held a long spear in his hand and he had a large sword in a sheath by his side and a man went before him with a shield. What is a shield? It is a great piece of iron, or bronze, like a large tray, which men used to hold before their faces in battle to prevent the arrows hurting their faces.

The giant Goliath thought that no one could kill him. Every day he used to call out with a loud voice, "Will one of the Israelites come and fight with me? If he is able to kill me, then all the Philistines will obey the king of Israel; but if I kill him, then the Israelites must obey the Philistines. Is there any man that will fight with me?"

Would any of the Israelites fight with the giant?

No, not one. When Saul heard the Philistine giant, he was frightened and all the Israelites were frightened. They all thought they would be killed, if one of them fought with the giant. And do you think that if one of them had fought with him he would have been killed? Could not God have helped the Israelite to conquer?

Where was David? Was he among the tents of Israel? No, he was feeding his father's sheep, but David's three elder brothers were in the tents.

One day, old Jesse said to David, "Go to the tents of Israel and see how your brothers are. Take with you some corn and ten loaves, as a present for your brothers.

So David rose up very early and left his sheep with another shepherd and took the corn and bread with him and went a long way till he came to the hill where the tents of the Israelites were. Then he ran to look for his brothers. As he was talking with his brothers, he heard a man speaking in a very loud voice, saying, "Who is able to fight with me?" It was the giant Goliath. David had never heard the giant speak these words before, but the people who were near David told him about the giant and they said, "King Saul has promised to give any man who kills the giant a great many things as a reward."

David was surprised that people would be afraid of fighting with the giant, because he knew that God could help an Israelite to conquer him. He knew that the gods of the Philistines could not help them, because they were only idols; so David said,

"Who is this Philistine, that he should speak in this manner to the people of God?" And David felt in his heart that he would not be afraid to fight with the giant.

One of David's brothers heard what David said and he mocked him. "Why did you come here? Why did you not stay with your sheep?" But David answered his brother very meekly.

Very soon someone went and told Saul that a young man had come to the tents and that he said he would fight with the giant. So Saul asked the young man to be brought before him and David came to Saul. Saul had seen David before; but Saul had forgotten him. Saul was surprised that David, who was so young, should wish to fight with the giant and he said to him, "You are not able to fight against that Philistine. You are very young and he has been used to fighting." Then David answered, "Once when I was keeping my father's sheep, a lion came and took a lamb out of the flock. I went after the lion and fought him and took the lamb out of his mouth. When the lion tried to kill me I caught him by his hair and killed him. And once a bear came and I killed him too. I shall kill this Philistine, as I killed the lion and the bear. It was God who delivered me from the paw of the lion and of the bear and He will deliver me from the Philistine."

You see David was not proud of his strength. He knew that it was God who had helped him kill those beasts and he felt sure that God would help him to kill the giant.

Questions for Chapter 12

Where did the Philistines live? Where did they place their tents?
Who were on the other hill?
Who was Goliath? What did he call out every day?
Why would none of the Israelites fight against Goliath?

Why did David think that he could conquer Goliath?
Why did David leave his sheep?
Who sent for David to speak to him?
What had God helped David to do, when he was watching his sheep?

Scripture Verse

Real strength is found in the Lord.
'The Lord is my strength and song and is become my salvation.' - (Ps. 118:14).

Notes for Chapter 12

1. The teacher can easily show the child a room of this height or some other object.

* * * * * * * * * * *

CHAPTER 13
DAVID AND THE FIGHT OF FAITH

1 Sam. 17:38-54.

When Saul heard David speak these words, he told him to go and fight the giant. But David had no sword, or boat of iron, so Saul lent him his own armour and his own sword; he put a cap of bronze on David's head and dressed him in a coat of iron. But David was not used to wearing armour; so he said to Saul, "I cannot wear this armour," and he took it off again; neither would he take a sword, or a spear. He went to the brook and chose five smooth stones and put them in a bag that he had and took the bag with him and a cloth. You will hear what he did with the bag, stones and cloth. In the other hand he held a stick. Then David went to meet the giant.

The giant heard that one of the Israelites was ready to fight with him and he came near to David; a man with a shield went before him. When the giant looked and saw David, he was surprised; he had expected to see a great man like himself, dressed in armour and holding a spear in his hand. But David was very young and his face was rosy like a child's. He only wore a shepherd's dress and he held a stick in his hand.

The Philistine giant was angry when he saw him and cursed him and used very wicked words. Then he began to laugh at David and said, "Come to me and I will give your flesh to the birds and to the beasts to eat." But David was not afraid and he said to the giant, "You have a sword and a spear and a shield; but God will fight for me and He will help me to kill you and take your head from you and the beasts and the birds shall eat up the flesh of all the Philistines. Everybody shall see that the God of Israel is the true God and that He can save whom He pleases."

Then the Philistine giant came still nearer to David and David ran towards him quickly, putting his hand in his bag and drewing out a stone David put it in the sling that he had. Then holding one end of the sling he threw the stone out of it with all his strength. The stone hit the giant on the forehead. It sank into it and the giant fell upon the ground on his face.

Then David ran to the giant and taking the giant's sword out of its sheath, he cut off his head. When the Philistines saw what a great wonder God had done they were frightened and the Israelites shouted for they saw that their God fought for them. They ran after the Philistines and the Philistines tried to run away; but the Israelites overtook a great many of them and killed them. David showed the head of the Philistine to a great many of the Israelites and he kept the armour that the Philistine had worn.

Did David thank God for helping him to conquer the giant? Oh, yes; he sang God's praise and played upon his harp. David did not wish people to praise him; he wished everybody to praise

God.[1] He wished all the people to say, "How great God is! He helped the poor young shepherd to conquer the great giant."

Proud people wish to be praised; but people who love God wish people to praise God. If God helps you to be good you ought to praise God for helping you to be good; if you remember things you are taught, you ought to praise God for helping you to remember. What do you say in the Lord's Prayer about praising God? You say, "Hallowed be your name"; which means, "Let God's name be praised."

Questions for Chapter 13

What did Saul lend David to wear?
What mocking words did the giant speak?
How did David kill the giant?
What became of the rest of the Philistine soldiers after Goliath was dead?
Did David wish to be praised for killing the giant?
Whom did he wish to be praised?
What is the meaning of "Hallowed be Thy name?"

Scripture Verse

God's attitude towards pride and humility.
'But he giveth more grace. Wherefore he saith, God resisteth the proud, but giveth grace unto the humble.' - (James 4:6).

Notes for Chapter 13

1. Psalm 18:48,49.

CHAPTER 14
DAVID AND THE SPEAR 1

1 Sam. 17:55 to end; 18; 19:1-10.

Saul was very glad that David had killed the giant Goliath. David was brought to Saul, so that Saul might speak to him. He came in with the giant's head in his hand. Then Saul said to David, "Whose son are you, young man?" And David answered, "I am the son of Jesse, who lives at Bethlehem."

While Saul was talking to David, there was a person standing near, whom you have not heard of before; it was the son of Saul. He was a grown-up man, very brave and very good; his name was Jonathan; he was a prince because he was the king's son.

Jonathan began to love David very much indeed. What could make Jonathan love David so much? I think he loved David because David was so brave and so good. David had also a very sweet look. Still it was God who made Jonathan love David so much. Jonathan told David that he loved him and they both promised always to be kind to each other. Jonathan gave his own clothes to David and wore other clothes and he also gave him his sword and his bow.

Saul told David that he must not go back to live with his father again, but that he must stay with him. So David and Jonathan saw each other very often. How much that must have pleased them, for friends like to be together.

Perhaps you think that David was now very happy. But there was one thing that soon happened to make him sad. I will tell you what it was.

After the giant had been killed in the battle, the Israelites went back to their homes and did not live in tents any more and Saul and Jonathan and David, went to the place where the king lived. As they were going along they saw a great many women with harps in their hands and these women played as they went and sang and danced. They were singing about David and how he had killed the Philistines and they said in their song that David had killed a great many more men than Saul. These are the words they sang, "Saul has slain his thousands and David his ten thousands."

Do you think that David liked to hear these songs? No. David did not wish to be praised. He wished God to be praised. He would have liked to hear the women say that God had helped a poor shepherd to kill the giant.

But when Saul heard these songs he was very angry, for he wished to be praised and he could not bear to hear David praised more than himself. "What," thought Saul, "do they say that David has killed more Philistines than I have and that he is braver than I am?" How wicked Saul was! He was envious; he was like Joseph's brothers and he was like Cain!

Then Saul thought, "Perhaps David is the man who is to be king instead of me?" Saul remembered that Samuel had told him that God had chosen a better man than he was to be king.

Did Saul guess right? Yes.

Then Saul hated David and wished to kill David. Saul had these wicked thoughts in his mind when he came back to his own house. Instead of thanking God for His kindness in having helped the Israelites to conquer the Philistines, he was thinking how he could kill David.

The next day after Saul had come home, God let the evil spirit come into him again. David saw that Saul was ill and unhappy. How did David try to make him well?

He took his harp, as he used to do and began to play sweet music. Now Saul had a spear in his hand and thought to himself, "I will throw this at David and it shall go through his body."

But David saw the javelin coming and he slipped out of the way; so that Saul did not hurt him. Then Saul threw it at him again, but he could not hurt David. God took care of David. Everyone but Saul loved David and this made Saul hate him still more.

David behaved so well, that Saul could not find any fault in him, for which he could punish him. Then Saul told David to take some men and to go and fight against the Philistines. Why did Saul send David to fight? Saul hoped that the Philistines would kill David in battle. David went and killed a great many Philistines, but no one hurt him. Everybody praised him more and called him brave. Saul grew angrier. At last Saul told all his servants to kill him; but they loved David and would not kill him. Still Jonathan was afraid in case some wicked person listen to Saul and kill David; so Jonathan told David to hide himself, while he begged his father to forgive him. So Jonathan said to his father, "Why do you wish to kill David? What has he done? Did he not once kill the giant? Then you were glad; why are you angry with him now?"

It was kind of Jonathan to speak up for David. It is kind of children to speak up for each other when they are in trouble. Saul promised that he would not have David killed. Then Jonathan called David and brought him to Saul and David was with him as he used to be.

But soon Saul began to hate David again and the evil spirit was on him still. Then David played on his harp to make him well. Saul had a spear in his hand and he threw it at David, but David slipped out of the way and the spear stuck in the wall.

Now David was afraid of staying anymore with Saul and he ran away that night.

He did not go back to his father, for Saul would have looked for him there and would have found him; but he hid himself in a great many places. You will hear of many sad things that will happen to poor David.

But God loved him and took care of him.

But Saul was miserable, for he was proud and envious, like Satan.

I wish you to love one another and not to want people to notice you. I hope you will not envy one another, but be glad when other children are praised.

Questions for Chapter 14

Who was Jonathan?
What first made Saul hate David?
What did Saul wish to do to David?
What did Saul throw at David?
Why did Saul send him to fight against the Philistines?
What did Saul instruct his servants to do to David?
Why did they not kill him?
Who begged Saul to be kind to David?
Did Saul promise that he would not try to kill David?
Did Saul keep his promise?
How did he try to kill him?
Where did David go?

Scripture Verse

The Godly way is to put others first before ourselves.
'Let nothing be done through strife or vainglory; but in lowliness of mind let each esteem other better than themselves' - (Phil 2:3).

CHAPTER 15
DAVID AND THE CAVE
1 Sam. 24

When David ran away from Saul, he was obliged to leave his dear friend Jonathan. David and Jonathan kissed each other and shed many tears when they parted; but Jonathan chose to stay with his father, King Saul. It was right of Jonathan to stay with his father. Where did David hide himself? There were very high hills in Canaan and there were large caves in these hills.

Very few people lived among these hills; but sheep fed upon the fresh grass that grew on them and goats leaped on the tops of the hills.

David was not alone. His brothers came to him, besides a great many poor people. These people liked to be with David, to help him, because Saul had wanted his servants to kill David. But these people were friends to David. David had God for his friend, too.

David and his friends lived together in a large cave; for some caves are very large and will hold as many people as you see in church on Sunday.

How did poor David and his friends get food? Kind people gave them food, for God made some people love David and be kind to him. Saul was very angry when he heard that anyone was kind to David. Saul used to tell people that David was wicked and that David wished to kill him. Was that true? No. Some people believed what Saul said and thought that David was really wicked so they mocked and abused David when they saw him.

Poor David! It made him sad to thing that people believed that he wanted to kill Saul. But it was a comfort to David to think that God knew that he did not want to kill Saul. So David used to comfort himself by praying to God. David had his harp with him in the cave;[1] he often sang psalms and praised God for keeping him from being hurt, though so many people were watching to kill him.[2]

David did not always live in the same cave, in case wicked people would tell Saul where he was hiding. So David sometimes hid himself among the thick trees in the wood and sometimes in one cave and sometimes in another.

Saul took a great many soldiers and came to look for David among the hills, but God did not let Saul find him. Saul said to the people he met, "Have you seen David and his men! If you love me, you will tell me where he is, for David wants to kill me." Then some people would tell Saul, "He is in the cave in that hill:" but when Saul got to the place he could not find David, for David heard that Saul was looking for him and he moved on to another cave. Saul was almost tired of looking for David, when something happened which you will like to hear.

Are caves dark inside, or light? Very dark. Because, though there is a hole to go in at, there are no windows to let in the light. One day David was in a very large cave with his men, when Saul and his men passed that way. Saul did not know that David was in the cave. Had he known it, he and his soldiers would have killed David and all his friends. But Saul saw the cave and he wished to go into it to sleep for a little while; so he left his men outside and came in quite alone. David and his men saw him come in, but Saul did not see David and his men, because they were in the dark parts of the cave.

How surprised David was to see Saul! David and his men remained quite quiet and Saul lay down to rest himself. Then David's men said to him in a low voice, "Now you can kill Saul if you wish it." Would David kill Saul? "No," said David, "I will not hurt the man whom God made king." And David would not let his men hurt Saul; but he went gently up to Saul as he lay asleep and cut off a piece of his clothes.

Why did he do this? You will soon find out the reason.

After a little while Saul rose up and went out of the cave and he and his men went on looking for David among the hills. Then David came out of the cave and called in a loud voice after Saul, "My Lord, the king." Then Saul looked behind him and David bowed himself down to the ground. How surprised Saul must now have been to see David? Then David spoke very meekly to Saul and said, "Why do you think that I wish to kill you? You came into the cave where I was and some people advised me to kill you; but I would not do it." Then David held up the piece of Saul's clothes that he had cut off. "Look, my father," said David, "at this; I cut it off. Could I not have killed you? Yes, I could; but I would not. Why, then, do you hunt after me? The Lord will keep me safe and will not let you hurt me."

When David had finished speaking, Saul said, "Is that your voice, my son David?" And Saul began to weep. He had once loved David and when he saw how good David was, he felt that he had been wicked; but he did not feel sorry that he had offended God.

"Yes," said Saul, "I see that you are much better than I am and that you do not wish to kill me and I know that you will be king one day."

So Saul did not try to kill David that day and he left off looking for David and went home with his men to his own house.

But David did not go and live with Saul, for he could not trust him. Once before Saul had promised Jonathan that he would not try to kill David again and yet he had broken his promise and David knew that perhaps he would soon try to kill him again. So David went back to his cave.

Saul was not sorry that he had offended God by his wickedness; Saul did not ask God to forgive him and to give him the Holy Spirit; so Satan would soon make him do wicked things again.

Now when you have been naughty, will you pray to God to forgive you and will you ask Him to put His Spirit in you? If you do not ask God to make you good, the devil will make you more and more wicked.

Questions for Chapter 15

Where did David hide himself?
Who went with David?
What did Saul tell people that David wanted to do?
What was David's comfort in his trouble?
Why could not Saul see David in the cave, when he came in one day by accident?
Why could David and his men see Saul?
Why did David cut off a piece of Saul's clothes?
Why would David not kill Saul?
How did Saul behave when David had come out of the cave and had spoken to him?
Why did not David go and live with Saul again?

Scripture Verse

God's promise to forgive if we admit our sins.

'If we confess our sins, he is faithful and just to forgive us our sins and to cleanse us from all unrighteousness. If we say that we have not sinned, we make him a liar and his word is not in us.' - (1 John 1:9,10).

Notes for Chapter 15

1. Ps. 57:8. 2. Ps. 54:6,7.

CHAPTER 16
DAVID AND THE SPEAR 2

1 Sam. 26.

You know that Saul had left off looking for David, after David had spoken to him. But Saul soon began to hate David again. One day some wicked men came to him and said, "We can tell you where David has hidden himself." Was it not very unkind of the men to tell Saul where poor David was? David had done them no harm, yet they behaved in this manner to him. Saul was glad to hear where David was and he took a great many soldiers with him and went to the place where he heard David was. Saul did not know the very place where David was, but he knew that David was hidden in some place near.

Saul ordered his men to set up their tents on a hill and to dig a deep ditch all round the tents so that nobody might come to the tents to hurt them. In the night Saul and his men would sleep in their tents and in the daytime they would look for David.

David heard that Saul was coming to look for him. How sorry David must have been to hear this! He could scarcely believe it; so he sent some men to go and look, to see whether Saul had really come and the men came back and told David that they had seen his tents on the hill.

Then David went with some of his friends near the place where the tents were and he said to his friends, "Who will go with me among the tents?" And one of David's friends said, "I will go with you." Then David and his friend went in the night and walked among the tents; but no one saw them or heard them; for all the people were fast asleep, for God had made them sleep. Even the people whom Saul had ordered to watch, to prevent anybody coming, even they had fallen asleep. God did not choose that David would be hurt; therefore He made the people sleep.

David got over the great ditch that had been dug, for there was nobody watching near to hinder him.

Into which of these tents do you think David went? Into the tent of Saul. He found him sleeping on his bed and by his pillow he saw his spear stuck into the ground and a jug of water and he saw other people, who ought to have watched him, asleep around him.

Saul did not know that David was so near him, looking at him as he slept. Then David's friend said to him, "Let me take this spear and kill Saul; I will pierce his body through in a moment."

Would David kill Saul? "No," said David, "do not kill him; it would be very wicked to kill the man whom God has made king. When God decided he should die, God will make him die, but I will not kill him. Only take the jug of water and the spear and let us go."

So they took the jug of water and the spear and they went away from the tents, and nobody woke while they were passing.

Why did David take the jug and the spear? You remember why he had once cut off some of Saul's clothes. It was for the same reason he now took the jug and spear. He wished to show Saul that he had been near his bed while he was asleep and that he might have killed him if he had chosen to.

Then David went down the hill where Saul's tents were and went up another hill; so there was a great way between Saul and him. Then David cried out with a very loud voice to the men that were sleeping round king Saul and said, "Why did you let people come near the king while he was asleep?"

You know why they had not watched; God had made them fall asleep.

Then David showed the people the king's spear and the jug of water.

When Saul heard David's voice, he remembered it and wept. He said, "Is that your voice, my son David?"

And David said, "It is my voice, my Lord, Oh, king. Why do you go on looking for me? What wickedness have I done? Have any wicked men told you that I wish to hurt you?"

Then Saul said, "I have sinned. Go to your home again. I will never hurt you again, because you did not kill me today when you might have done it. I have been very wicked."

Was Saul very sorry for his wickedness? Oh, no! He did not pray to God to forgive him and make him good.

Then David said, "Here is the king's spear. Send one of your servants to fetch it."

Why would not David bring the spear to Saul himself? He could not trust Saul; he was not sure that Saul would not kill him.

Saul said, "Blessed be you, my son David." And then Saul went home, but David went into the part of Canaan where the Philistines lived, that Saul might not be able to hurt him and God made the Philistines kind to David.

David ought not to have gone to live with the Philistines, because they worshipped idols. David ought to have trusted in God to keep him safe among the caves and hills.

When Saul went home this time, did he pray to God to keep him from Satan and from hating David again? Let me tell you again that this is the way to grow good. It is not enough to say, "I will be good; I will not do that naughty thing any more"; you should always pray to God to keep you from wickedness. For Satan is a great deal stronger than you and unless God is with you, Satan can make you do wicked things. So if you wish not to listen to Satan, ask God to put His Holy Spirit into you.[1]

Questions for Chapter 16

Did Saul come to look for David again, after David's kindness in not killing him in the cave?
Did David go to Saul's tents in the night, or in the day?
Why did Saul and his soldiers sleep so soundly?
Why did David take away Saul's spear and his jug?
Why did not David bring them back to Saul himself?
Why did David go and live with the Philistines?
Why was it wrong in David to go and live with the Philistines?

Scripture Verse

How to deal with Satan.
'Submit yourselves therefore to God. Resist the devil and he will flee from you.' - (James 4:7).

Notes for Chapter 16

1. 1 John 5:18.

* * * * * * * * * *

CHAPTER 17
DAVID AND THE DEATH OF SAUL

1 Sam. 31

Where did David at last go to hide himself from Saul? To the land of the Philistines; they were wicked people, who worshipped idols, yet God made them kind to David and to his men.

When Saul heard that David was gone to the Philistines, he went to look for him no more; because if Saul had gone to them, they would have tried to kill him.

The time was now almost come when Saul must die. I will now tell you how he died. You know that the Philistines hated the people of Israel and used to fight against them. One day the king of the Philistines called a great many of his soldiers together and took them to a place in the land of Canaan, where they might fight with the Israelites. When Saul heard they were come, he took his soldiers and went to fight against them. Saul's good son Jonathan went with his father to the battle.

The Philistines and the Israelites fought together upon some hills. Who do you think conquered? The Philistines conquered. God was angry with the Israelites and He did not help them to conquer. The Israelites ran away from the Philistines; even Saul and Jonathan, though they were brave, ran away and the Philistines ran after them and they killed Jonathan. And did they kill Saul? This was the way in which Saul died. Some men with bows and arrows shot at him and some of the arrows went into Saul's body so that he could not run away any more; yet Saul was not killed by the arrows, he was only badly hurt.

When Saul found that he could not run away, he was very unhappy, for he was afraid that the Philistines would soon get hold of him and treat him very cruelly; so he wished very much to die before they overtook him. Then Saul said to one of his soldiers, "Take your sword and run it through my body."

Would it have been right of the soldier to kill Saul? If your brother were to ask you to kill him, might you kill him? No, you might not. God has said, "You shall not kill."

Saul's soldier would not kill Saul. Then Saul took his own sword and fell upon the point of it; so it ran through his body and he died. Was it right of Saul to kill himself? Oh, no, he should have waited till God made him die. It is very wicked of people to kill themselves. People who love God wait till God takes away their breath.

When Saul was dead, the soldier who refused to kill Saul when Saul asked him, fell upon his sword and died with him. The soldier saw Saul do a wicked thing and he did the same.

The Philistines went on running after the Israelites all that day and they killed a great many.

The next day the Philistines went to the hills, where they had been fighting to look at the dead people who were lying there. They found Saul's dead body and Jonathan's dead body. How pleased they were to find that the king and his brave son were dead! But how shamefully they treated their bodies! They cut off Saul's head; they stripped off Saul's clothes of iron and bronze (his armour) and they sent his head and his armour to all the places where the Philistines lived and they praised their idols and said that their idols were greater than the God of Israel because their idols had helped them to conquer the Israelites. Then they took Saul's armour and put it in one of the houses where they worshipped idols and they fastened his body to the wall of one of the idol's houses that everybody might see it. And they fastened Jonathan's body to the same place. Was this not a sad thing to happen to poor Jonathan? But God loved Jonathan and blessed him forever.

Questions for Chapter 17

Who shot king Saul with their arrows?
How did Saul kill himself?
Why was it wicked for people to kill themselves?
What did the Philistines do with Saul's head and his armour?
And what did they do with his body and with Jonathan's body?
Whom did the Philistines praise after they had conquered Saul?

Scripture Verse

Faith is to leave our fate in the hands of God.

'...be thou faithful unto death and I will give thee a crown of life.' - (Rev. 2:10).

SECTION 2

2 SAMUEL

Introduction

As 1 Samuel closes, we learn that Samuel has died and with his death comes the end of the time of the Judges. We learn of the sad tale of the death of King Saul, a man who stepped outside of God's blessing. Now the way is open for David to become King, just as God had willed.

2 Samuel shows us that through David, God makes the Israelites an even greater, stronger and more prosperous people. However, it also records that even David was disobedient. The book shows us how this led to a weakness in his reign which was to cause division and rebellion. However, overall in David, there is new hope and a King by which all other Kings of God's people would be judged.

Some Suggestions for Study

As you read each chapter, think of one person in the story who said or did something which was either pleasing or displeasing to God. Think about the effect that this action had on the people of God. Write down one way in which you hope to affect someone positively and ask God to give you opportunities to do it.

CHAPTER 18
DAVID AND THE PROMISE FULFILLED

2 Sam.2:1-4; 5:1-3.

Some of the Israelites heard where the Philistines had fastened the bodies of Saul and Jonathan and these kind men travelled all night to the place and took their bodies down from the wall and burned them and buried their bones under a tree.

Where was David all this time? He was in the land of the Philistines. He knew that Saul and Jonathan had been fighting a battle and he longed to know who had conquered. At last a man who had been at the battle, came to David, to tell him about it. The man bowed down to David and David said, "Where do you come from?"

And the man said, "I come from the tents of Israel."

Then David said, "Please tell me what has happened."

And the man said, "The Israelites have run away and many are dead and Saul and Jonathan his son are dead also."

The men thought that David would have been very glad to hear that Saul was dead. But was David glad? No, he still loved Saul and he was sorry too that the Philistines should have conquered him, because he knew that the Philistines would praise their idols and speak against the God of Israel and David loved God so much, that he wished everybody to praise Him. And David was very sorry for Jonathan, his friend. He would never see his face again in this world.

David sang a sweet song about Saul and Jonathan. He said that Saul and Jonathan had been like eagles and lions, they had been so brave; he said they had lived together and had died together. And then he said in his song, "I am distressed for you, my brother Jonathan; your love to me was wonderful." He called Jonathan his brother, because he had been very kind to him.

David did not speak of Saul's wickedness, but only of his bravery; for he did not like to speak against the king.

Now the time was come when David was to be king. God put it into the hearts of the Israelites to ask David to be their king. God had promised that David should be king and God kept His promise and made him king.

God always keeps His promises. What did God once promise Abraham? That he should have a son and that his children's children should live in the land of Canaan. Did God keep these promises? Oh, yes! What has God promised you? To give you His Spirit, if you ask Him and I know He will keep His promise to you. He will keep all His promises. He has promised if you have His Spirit, to give you a crown of glory. I hope that you will ask Him for His Holy Spirit.

David praised God on his harp for keeping His promise to him; for taking him from keeping sheep, to make him king over all the land. David wished to be a good king and to do all that God told him and to teach all his people to love God. He knew that God would bless him and keep him from all harm.

Questions for Chapter 18

Who told David that Saul was dead?
Was David glad when he heard that Saul was dead?
How did he show his grief?
Whom did the Israelites make king, now Saul was dead?
Had God ever promised David that he should be king?
What promise had God once made to Abraham?
Did God keep that promise?
What promise has God made to you?

Scripture Verse

God's will fulfil his promises.

'Let us hold fast the profession of our faith without wavering; (for he *is* faithful that promised;).' - (Heb. 10:23)

* * * * * * * * * *

CHAPTER 19

DAVID AND THE ARK ON ZION

2 Sam. 5:7-11; 1 Chron. 13; 15; 16.

At last David was made king, as God had promised. I will tell you the name of the city in which he lived; it was Jerusalem. David was born at Bethlehem and there he kept sheep, but when he was king he lived at Jerusalem.

Jerusalem was a beautiful city. There were a great many hills in it. Do you not think hills very beautiful? One of the hills was called Mount Zion.

David asked for some men to build him a house upon Mount Zion. A king's house is called a palace. David's palace was on Mount Zion.

David loved God very much and so he thought he should like God's ark to be very near his palace.

Where was the ark?

You remember that the ark was once at Shiloh and that the Philistines took it in battle and that they sent it back to the Israelites; but the ark never was taken back to Shiloh again. God would not let the wicked people who lived in Shiloh have His ark any more.

The ark had been kept in a man's house; David knew where it was and he went himself to fetch it. A great many priests came with David and a great many people, who played on musical instruments, such as harps and trumpets and other instruments called cornets and cymbals and psalteries and some people who sang sweet psalms in the praise of God. So they brought the ark from the man's house to Jerusalem, on Mount Zion. David was dressed in a white ephod and all the singers and players of music were dressed in white and the priests were dressed in white.

David played upon his harp and he went with the players and singers and the ark came afterwards with the priests.

How beautiful it was to see all these men in white and to hear them praising God!

Would not the sight have made you think of the angels of God in heaven?

A great many of the Israelites came to see this beautiful sight. They saw their king praising God upon his harp. Oh, how glad David felt that day!

The ark was taken up the hill called Mount Zion. There were walls all round the top of Mount Zion and large gates; the gates were opened wide to let the king come in and the ark, which was the throne of the Lord.[1] David had prepared a place made of curtains for the ark to be placed in. He had not brought the old tabernacle to Mount Zion; but he had made a new tabernacle, close to his own palace.[2] There the priests placed the ark and David instructed the singers to sing a psalm that he had written, beginning "Give thanks unto the Lord."

David also offered some sacrifices upon Mount Zion and David blessed all the people that stood around. Before the people went home, he instructed that every man and every woman should have some bread and some meat and a little bottle of wine. Was not this very kind of David?

David was very glad that God's ark was near his own palace. He instructed the singers and players of music to sing and play every day near the ark. He instructed them to sing in the night also; some used to sing in the day and some used to sing in the night.[3] They sang by turns. The angels in heaven can sing night and day without resting, but these singers could not do so. When David was in his palace, he could hear them singing God's praise; even at night, if he lay awake upon his bed, he could hear those sweet songs.

David wrote the psalms himself; God's Spirit inspired what he said.[4] He sang the psalms to his own harp and he wrote them down and sent them to the singers, that they might sing near the ark.

David did not always stay in his palace on Mount Zion. He was often obliged to go out to fight against the Philistines and other wicked people and God helped David and his men to conquer them all. Then David used to return to Mount Zion and sing psalms to God for having helped him to conquer.[5]

Questions for Chapter 19

In what city did David live when he was king?
What was the name of the hill in Jerusalem on which David's house was built?
Why did David wish to have the ark near his palace?
Where had the ark been kept since the Philistines had sent it back?
Who went before the ark as it was being taken to Mount Zion?
How did David show his joy as he went along?
What commands did David give to the singers?
In what tabernacle did David place the ark?

Scripture Verse

It is good to praise the Lord.
'Let every thing that hath breath praise the Lord. Praise ye the Lord.' - (Ps. 150:6).

Notes for Chapter 19

1. Ps. 24:7. 2. 2 Chronicles 1:3,4. 3. Ps. 134:1. 4. 2 Sam. 23:1,2. 5. 2 Sam. 22:1.

* * * * * * * * * *

CHAPTER 20
DAVID AND THE GRATEFUL DESIRE

1 Chron. 17

One day when David was sitting in his beautiful palace he said to his friend Nathan, "I live in a fine house, but God's ark is placed under curtains." David wished to build a beautiful house for God's ark.

Nathan, David's friend, was a very wise, very good man and he advised David to build a house for the Lord.

In the night God spoke to Nathan and said to him, "Go, tell David not to build me a house; I am pleased with David for wishing to build it, but I do not choose him to build me one, because he has fought so many battles and killed so many people; but I will give David a son, who shall build me a house; but David shall go on fighting battles and I will bless David always."

God was not displeased with David for fighting battles, only He did not choose that he should build Him a house.

Then Nathan came to David in the morning and told him what God had said.

David was very pleased to hear that God would bless him and that He would give him a son who should build a house for God. So David went to thank God for His kind promises.

David said, "Oh, Lord, how kind you have been to me! And will you still go on blessing me? I do not deserve such kindness. How can I thank you enough? Pray go on blessing me and loving me!"

God liked David's prayer. David was not proud. He was amazed that God should be so kind to him and that He should have taken him from being a shepherd to be the king over Israel. He was full of wonder that God would promise to bless him always and to bless his son; for David knew that he deserved nothing, for he was but a poor sinner.

Has not God been kind to you? And has He not promised to take you to live with Him if you ask Him? Did you ever wonder to yourself why God was so kind to you? It was not because you are good, because you are full of sin. It was because God is so good and loves to bless people.

Questions for Chapter 20

What grateful wish came into David's heart?
Why would not God allow David to build a house for the ark?
Who told David he might not build it?
Who was to build God's house?
Did David deserve that God should bless him always?
Why does God bless you?

Scripture Verse

God desires the best for us.
'For God so loved the world, that he gave his only begotten Son, that whosoever believeth in him should not perish, but have everlasting life.' - (John 3:16).

CHAPTER 21
DAVID AND URIAH'S WIFE

2 Sam. 11.

Was David a good man? Oh, yes! he loved God and tried to please Him. What made David good? God's Holy Spirit. God put His Spirit into his heart; yet still there was wickedness in David's heart, as well as goodness. Satan, too, used to tempt David to do wicked things. Sometimes David did not pray to God to keep him from Satan and then David used to listen to what Satan said. Shall you not be very sorry to hear of a wicked thing that David did?

I am now going to tell you about a time that David displeased the Lord.

Once David's men went out to fight against some wicked people who lived near Canaan. David did not go himself to fight this time, but he told a man named Joab to take the people to fight. This Joab was called David's captain because he took soldiers with him to battle and told them when to fight.

So David stayed at Jerusalem. I do not know why he did not go out to fight himself; I am afraid that he was idle and liked better staying at home to eat and drink and rest himself. It is very wrong to be idle. Did you ever hear this hymn;

'Satan finds some mischief still
For idle hands to do?'

One day, when it was hot, David lay upon his bed and when it grew cool he got up and walked on the top of his house, which was flat like a table. As he was walking there he looked down and saw a woman, whom he liked very much as soon as he saw her. David wished to have her as his wife; so he sent his servants to ask what her name was. They came back and told him that her name was Bath-she-ba and that she was married to a man called Uriah.

Could David have Bathsheba as his wife, if she was married to Uriah? Oh no, David could not take her away from Uriah to be his wife; that would have been wicked; for God has said in the ten commandments, "You shall not commit adultery." David ought to have prayed to God to keep him from thinking of Bathsheba any more; but he went on thinking of her and wishing that she could be his wife and he thought, "If Uriah was dead, then Bathsheba could be my wife." Then he wished that Uriah were dead. Now Uriah was a very brave and good man and he was gone with the captain Joab a great way off, to fight against some wicked people.

David wished that Uriah might be killed in the battle. Was that not very wicked? God said in the ten commandments, "You shall not kill," and we must not even wish a person to be killed.

At last a very wicked plan came into David's heart. I will tell you what David did. David wrote a letter to Joab the captain and this is what he wrote: " When you take the people out to fight, let Uriah stand in a place where the wicked people will be able to shoot him."

How could David write such a letter? David sent the letter to Joab. Ought Joab to have done this wicked thing? Oh no, he ought not to have obeyed David. But Joab was a very wicked man, so he determined to do as the king had told him.

Soon afterwards Joab took his soldiers to fight against a great city with walls all round it and he told Uriah to go with some of the soldiers very near the walls of the city and some of the men of the city shot arrows from the walls and killed poor Uriah.

Then Joab sent a man to tell king David at Jerusalem that Uriah was dead.

Was David sorry when he heard that Uriah was killed? He pretended to be sorry, but he felt glad in his heart. You know why he was glad. Now Bathsheba could be his wife; so he sent for Bathsheba and he married her and she came and lived with him in his palace.

But God was displeased at what David had done.

Questions for Chapter 21

Did David always take his soldiers to battle himself?
Who was David's captain?
How did David first see Bathsheba?
What wicked wish came into his heart?
Why did David wish that Uriah was dead?
What commandment do we break when we wish people to die?
What wicked letter did David write?
What did David instruct Joab to do with Uriah?
Why was David glad when Uriah was dead?

Scripture Verse

God says adultery is wrong.
'Neither shalt thou commit adultery.' - (Deu. 5:18).

CHAPTER 22
DAVID AND NATHAN'S VISIT

2 Sam. 12:1-14.

One day Nathan, who was a prophet, came to David.

God had told Nathan what David had done.

Nathan began by telling David a story. He said, "There were two men in one city; the one was rich and the other was poor; the rich man had a great many sheep, the poor man had only one little lamb, which he had taken care of since it was first born. He fed it and gave it drink out of his own cup, he nursed it and loved it as one of his children. One day a visitor came to the rich man's house and the rich man sent for the poor man's lamb, killed it and prepared it for dinner for his visitor." Then said Nathan, "What shall be done to the rich man?"

And David felt very angry with the rich man and he said to Nathan, "He shall die and give the poor man four lambs instead of the one which he took."

Then Nathan said to David, "You are the man!"

What did Nathan mean? Was David the man who had taken the poor man's lamb? No, David had not taken a lamb, but he had taken Uriah's wife and that was much more wicked. Nathan had told him this story to show him what a wicked thing he had done. Did not David deserve to die?

Nathan said to David, "God has been very kind to you and made you king. Why have you disobeyed his commandments? God will punish you for your wickedness. Your children shall fight each other and kill each other and behave very wickedly to you as long as you live."

David was very sorry when he heard that God was angry

with what he had done and he said, "I have sinned against the Lord."

Then Nathan said, "God has forgiven you; you shall not die."

David was really sorry for what he had done. He was not like Saul, who only cared for the punishment; he was most sorry because he had displeased God.

David played a very sad psalm on his harp and he gave it to the singers to sing near the ark.

He asked God in his psalm to wash out his sins. These were some of David's words: "Wash me and I shall be whiter than snow. Create in me a clean heart, Oh, God and renew a right spirit within me.[1]

You see that David prayed to God to forgive him and God did forgive him. God would not send David to hell, but He would forgive him, because Jesus had promised to die for him some day upon the cross. Yet still God would punish David while he was alive, that all people might know that God hated wickedness.

I hope that you will often pray to God to keep you from Satan; but whenever you have done a naughty thing I hope you will feel sorry and that you will ask God to forgive you, I know He will forgive you, because Jesus died on the cross for sinners.[2]

If you do not feel sorry, then you should ask God to make you feel sorry; for it is God's spirit that makes people sorry for their sins.

Questions for Chapter 22

Why did Nathan tell David the story of the poor man's lamb?
Did David know the meaning at first?
How did David find out the meaning?
What punishment did God say that David should have?

Was David sorry for what he had done?
What did he say to Nathan?
What did he say to God in his psalms?
Did God forgive him?
Why did God forgive him?
Why did God punish him?
Who makes people feel sorry for their sins?

Scripture Verse

God's promise to forgive if we admit our sins.
'If we confess our sins, he is faithful and just to forgive us our sins and to cleanse us from all unrighteousness. If we say that we have not sinned, we make him a liar and his word is not in us.' - (1 John 1:9-10).

Notes for Chapter 22

1. Ps. 51. 2. 1 John 2:1,2.

* * * * * * * * * *

CHAPTER 23
DAVID AND THE PUNISHMENT

2 Sam. 15.

You remember that God said He would punish David, though He had forgiven him.

David had a great many children and some of them were very wicked when they grew up. I cannot tell you about all his bad children, but I will tell you of one called Absalom. He was a very proud young man. He was very handsome and he had beautiful hair and he was very vain about his good looks. He also told lies and he even killed one of his brothers who had offended him. When David heard how Absalom had killed his brother, he was angry with him for a long time and would not see him; but at last he let him come to his palace, kissed him and forgave him. David ought never to have allowed Absalom to come to Jerusalem again after he had killed his brother; but David was too fond of Absalom.

Yet Absalom did not love his father David. He wished to be king instead of David and so he behaved very kindly to all the people in Jerusalem, that they might love him better than they loved his father and make him king. He used sometimes to kiss the poor people that he saw and tell them that if he were king he would be very kind to them.

This kind way of behaving made the people love Absalom, for they thought that he really cared for them. How very sly and deceitful Absalom was! God did not love him.

When Absalom saw that many of the people loved him, he asked David's leave to go from Jerusalem into the country. David gave him leave. David did not know what a wicked plan Absalom had made. This was the wicked plan.

Absalom had instructed a great many men to wait till they heard the sound of a trumpet and when they heard it, to cry out, "Absalom is king!" So when Absalom had left Jerusalem and come into the country, he instructed the trumpet to be blown and a great many of the people called out, "Absalom is king!" and came to Absalom to be his soldiers.

Poor David was in Jerusalem and a messenger came and told him that Absalom had made himself king.

How grieved David was to hear this news! He could not bear to think that his son was so wicked as to make himself king. Then David thought of his own sin and he felt that he deserved to be punished. He knew that it was God who let all these sad things happen to him.

David would not stay in Jerusalem, for he thought that Absalom would soon come there and would perhaps kill him and his servants. So the king left his palace on Mount Zion, to go a great way off. There were many people in Jerusalem who loved David and they went with him.

First they crossed a little river that was outside Jerusalem and as they went over all the people wept. They wept to think that their dear king was obliged to leave his house and to wander about without a home.

Then David and his servants went up a high hill and David wept as he went up and he covered his head and he wore no shoes on his feet; he did these things to show he was unhappy and all the people with him did the same and wept as they went up. You see how much the people loved David.

And when David was come to the top of the hill he prayed to God. He knew that God would comfort him in his distress.

Questions for Chapter 23

What was the name of David's wicked son who killed his brother?
Did David forgive him?
Was it right to let him come home?
Why did Absalom behave very kindly to poor people?
What did Absalom instruct people to cry out when they heard the trumpet?
Why did David leave Jerusalem?
Where did David weep and pray?

Scripture Verse

God is always there in our time of need to comfort us.
'Yea, though I walk through the valley of the shadow of death, I will fear no evil: for thou art with me; thy rod and thy staff they comfort me.' - (Ps. 23:4).

CHAPTER 24
DAVID AND PATIENCE

2 Sam. 16:5-14; 17:27 to end.

Then David went on his sorrowful journey. Soon he met a very wicked man who hated him and who called David very bad names and even threw stones at David and his soldiers. This wicked man called David a child of the devil and said, "You killed Saul and his children and now God is punishing you for your wickedness."

Had David killed Saul or his children? Oh, no! The man told lies about David. But David had killed Uriah and God was punishing him for that sin.

One of David's friends said to him, "Do not let that wicked man call you names; let me go and take off his head."

But David said, "No, the Lord lets him curse me and I will not hinder him. My own son seeks to kill me. I am not surprised that this man curses me."

How meekly David behaved! This was the way that Jesus behaved to wicked people. You see what we should do when people are unkind and cruel to us. We ought not to give them rude answers, but we ought to think of the bad things we have done and behave meekly.

This wicked man went on cursing and throwing stones and dust at David and his soldiers.

At last David and his men came to a place where they rested themselves, for they were very tired. David and his soldiers travelled a long way. At last they crossed over the river Jordan. I believe they found some place where the water was not too deep. On the other side there was a place called a wilderness.

There were three very rich men who lived near the wilderness who heard of poor David and his men having come there and these rich men said, "They must be very hungry and thirsty and weary, in the wilderness"; so they brought David and his men a great many things; beds to rest their weary limbs upon, basins and cups to drink out of and sheep and vegetables, honey, butter, cheese and corn to eat. These rich men were very kind; God put it in their hearts to be kind to poor David in his distress.

While David was in the wilderness he often prayed to God and asked God to comfort him. David felt that he deserved to be punished; so he behaved very meekly. This is the way you should behave when you are punished for your faults. If you are really sorry, you will not be angry with the people who punish you; but when you are in disgrace you will pray to God to forgive you and to put His Spirit in your heart to make you good.

Questions for Chapter 24

How did a wicked man whom David met behave to David?
What false things did he say?
How did David bear his treatment?
Why was he so patient?
What did some rich men give to David and his men in the wilderness?
What made them so kind?

Scripture Verse

A sincere and humble heart is what God desires of us.

'For thou desirest not sacrifice; else would I give it: thou delightest not in burnt offering. The sacrifices of God are a broken spirit: a broken and a contrite heart, Oh, God, thou wilt not despise.' - (Ps. 51:16,17).

CHAPTER 25
DAVID AND THE TREE

2 Sam. 18:1-16.

David and his men lived in a city in the wilderness. The city had walls and gates.

Absalom soon heard where his father David was and he came after him with a great army. Absalom crossed over the river Jordan and instructed his men to set up their tents near the city where David was.

Then David saw that his wicked son meant to fight against him. So David one morning instructed his soldiers to go out of the city. David was going with them; but they begged him not to come in case he should be killed in the battle. These people loved him very much. Then the king said, "I will do as you think best." David did not wish to go to this battle, for he did not like to fight against Absalom.

David told the soldiers, before they went to battle, not to hurt Absalom; for David still loved his wicked son.

Absalom and his soldiers came out to fight against David's men. They fought in a wood. This was not a good place for fighting, for a great many people were knocked against the trees and bruised and killed.

Who do you think conquered? David's men - because God helped them. Absalom's men tried to run away and a great many of them were killed by the swords of David's men and still more were killed by the trees in the wood.

Now you shall hear what became of Absalom.

He rode upon a mule (which is a animal very much like a horse) and as he was riding he passed under a large tree, his handsome head was caught in the boughs.[1] The mule ran away and left him hanging by his head in the tree, with his feet lifted up from the earth.

One of David's soldiers saw him and went to the captain Joab and said, "Behold, I saw Absalom hanging in a tree."

Then Joab said, "And why did you not kill him? If you had I would have given you a great deal of silver and some clothes."

But the man answered, "If you would have given me a thousand pieces of silver I would not have hurt Absalom, for I heard the king command that no one should hurt him."

Then Joab went very quickly to the tree and he found Absalom still hanging there. So he took three darts and thrust them through Absalom's heart - just through the middle of his body and ten young men that were with Joab hurt him also with swords, or darts and killed him.

How frightened Absalom must have felt when he was hanging in the oak! I wonder whether he prayed to God to forgive him! Perhaps he did not wish to pray; for he did not love God. Perhaps he only felt frightened in case anyone should kill him. The darts must have hurt his body very much and must have covered him with blood. Did he not well deserve to feel pain? What pain had he made his father feel in his mind?

Joab took his body down from the tree, threw it into a great pit in the wood and laid a great heap of stones on the spot.

When Absalom was dead, Joab blew a trumpet to call back his soldiers from running after Absalom's soldiers; for now Absalom was dead the Israelites could stop fighting. Absalom's soldiers went back to their tents and Joab took his soldiers back to the city where David was.

But before Joab and his men went back, two men ran very fast to tell David what had happened.

How David longed to know whether Absalom was dead! David wished his men to conquer and yet he did not wish

Absalom to be killed. No, he would rather die himself than that Absalom should be killed.

Questions for Chapter 25

In what sort of places did David's soldiers fight against Absalom and his soldiers?
Did David fight?
Why not?
How was Absalom caught?
Why did not the first man who saw Absalom in the tree kill him?
How was he killed at last?
What was done with his body?
Why did Joab blow a trumpet after Absalom was dead?

Scripture Verse

Absalom suffered because of his actions.
'Be not deceived; God is not mocked: for whatsoever a man soweth, that shall he also reap. For he that soweth to his flesh shall of the flesh reap corruption; but he that soweth to the Spirit shall of the Spirit reap life everlasting.' - (Gal 6:7-8).

Notes for Chapter 25

1. It is not written that Absalom was caught by his hair (though this is generally supposed) but by his *head*. His head may have been jammed between forked boughs (branches).

CHAPTER 26
DAVID AND THE TWO MESSENGERS

2 Sam. 18:19 to end; 19:1-4.

David was sitting near the gates of the city in the wilderness. A man stood upon the top of the wall near the gate, to watch to see whether any person was coming into the city. Soon the watchman saw a man running and he cried out loud, "I see a man running alone." Then David said, "No doubt he brings some message." Soon afterwards the watchman cried out, "I see another man running alone." Then David said, "He also brings a message."

The first man was a young priest. He ran up to David and cried out, "All is well." He said all was well, because David's men had conquered. Then the priest fell down to the ground upon his face before the king and he thanked God for having let David's men conquer. Then the king said, "Is the young Absalom safe?" The priest knew that Absalom was dead, but he did not like to grieve David by telling him this sad news all at once, so he said, "There was a great deal of noise and confusion when Joab sent me here." This young priest loved David so much that he did not like to tell David what the noise was about.

Soon the other man came running up to David and he said, "God has punished the wicked people who fought against the king." Then the king said, "Is the young man Absalom safe?" And the messenger answered, "May all people who fight against the king be as Absalom now is!" The king knew that the man meant that Absalom was dead. How unhappy the king was when he heard this! He went into a room that was near the gate and he wept and said, "Oh, my son Absalom, my son, my son Absalom! Would God I had died for you, Oh, Absalom, my son, my son!"

When David's soldiers were coming back into the city, they

heard how much the king grieved for Absalom and they felt unhappy, too, because they loved the king. The king did not come out to meet them and to thank them for having fought for him, as he would have done if Absalom had not been killed; but he remained by himself and he covered his face and cried, "Oh, my son Absalom, my son, my son!"

I do not wonder that David was unhappy about Absalom. Could David hope that he was gone to heaven and that he should see him again one day? Oh, it is dreadful to be a wicked child! God cut off Absalom in the midst of his wickedness.

Jonathan died while he was young, but he was good and he went to heaven. I hope that none of you will die in wickedness, as Absalom did. Pray now to God, to make you love and obey Him and I know He will hear you. Why will He hear you? Because Jesus died for you.

Questions for Chapter 26

Where was David sitting during the battle?
Why didn't the first messenger tell David that Absalom was dead?
What did he tell him?
What did the second messenger say?
What did David say in his grief?
Why was the king so very unhappy that Absalom was dead?
How does God punish children who behave badly to their parents?

Scripture Verse

The promise to those who love the Lord.
'...If a man loves me, he will keep my words: and my Father will love him and we will come unto him and make our abode with him."' - (John 14:23).

CHAPTER 27
DAVID AND THE RETURN

2 Sam. 19.

Did not Absalom come to a very dreadful end? He died in the midst of his wickedness; for God curses children who behave ungratefully to their parents. How much David loved this wicked Absalom! He went on crying for him for some time. David knew why God had let him have such a wicked child. Do you know why? It was because David had killed Uriah. Yet God had forgiven David.

Now Absalom was dead, David could return to Jerusalem. The people who had said that Absalom was king now wished David to be king again. So David went over the River Jordan on his way back to Jerusalem. As he was on the other side of the river, a man came to David and threw himself down before him to ask his pardon. Who could this man be? It was the wicked man who had thrown stones and dust at David when he was unhappy.

Did David forgive him? Yes he did. Was that not kind of David? The man deserved to die, but David said to him, “You shall not die.” The man was not really sorry; only he did not dare to behave badly to David, now he was king again. God would punish that wicked man, though David forgave him. I hope that you will forgive people who behave rudely to you; God has said, that if we do not forgive He will not forgive us.

There was another man who came to see David before he crossed over the river. It was one of those rich men who had been kind to David in his distress and who had sent him the presents of beds, basins and food. He was an old man and David thanked him and asked him to come and live with him at

Jerusalem. The rich man said he was too old, but that he would like David to take his servant with him and he kissed the old man and blessed him. David was grateful; he was kind to people who had been so kind to him.

David was very glad to come back to Jerusalem. Do you know what made him most glad? It was because he wished to worship God near His ark and to hear all the people praising God. While David had been a great way from Jerusalem, he had often sighed and wept to think that he could not go to the house of the Lord,[1] for David loved God very much. David was pleased to see the priests offer sacrifices on the altar to God and to praise God himself for His goodness upon his harp.[2]

Questions for Chapter 27

To what city did David return after Absalom's death?
Who asked David's pardon on his way to Jerusalem?
Why did David forgive him?
How did David behave to an old man who had been kind to him?
What made David most glad when he returned to Jerusalem?

Scripture Verse

It is good to desire to be close to God.

'Blessed is the man whom thou choosest and causest to approach unto thee, that he may dwell in thy courts: we shall be satisfied with the goodness of thy house, even of thy holy temple.' - (Ps. 65:4).

Notes for Chapter 27

1. Compare with Ps. 42:3,4. 2. Compare with Ps. 43:4.

SECTION 3

1 & 2 KINGS

(Including references to 1 & 2 Chronicles)

Introduction

The books of 1 and 2 Kings continue the story of God's people under the rule of many Kings. 1 Kings tells us about the end of David's reign and how his son Solomon comes to the throne. God blesses Solomon and the nation becomes richer and stronger than it ever has been or ever will be. It is through Solomon that God allows the first magnificent temple to be built in Jerusalem.

However, after a promising start, Solomon turns away from God to worship false gods. When he dies, the Kingdom divides into two - Israel in the north and Judah in the south. The remainder of 1 Kings and 2 Kings tell the sad tale of the two kingdoms. Some of the kings are good and follow God's ways and others are bad and worship false gods. Eventually, first Israel and then Judah, are invaded by powerful nations and the people are taken away into exile as slaves.

Some Suggestions for Study

When you have read a chapter, think of something that God might wish to teach you through the story. Draw a sketch to illustrate this and write underneath a sentence or word which sums up what you have learned. Or you might like to take the Bible verse and draw something which links in with it.

CHAPTER 28
DAVID AND THE FAREWELL

1 Kings 1:32-40; 1 Chron. 28;29.

You remember the kind promise that God made to David. He had promised that David should have one good son, who should be king after David was dead, who should build a house for the Lord.

One of David's sons was good. God loved him and made him good. His name was Solomon. God told David that he was to be king after him. At last David grew very old and weak and he knew that he should die. So he wished to make Solomon king before he died. He instructed the high priest to pour oil upon his head and so the high priest anointed Solomon to be king.

Then David instructed his people to come together to a place in Jerusalem, that he might speak to them all before he died. When they were all come, the king stood up on his feet and said, "I once wished to build a house for the ark of God, but God would not let me build a house, because I had shed so much blood in battle, but He said that my son should build it."

Then David spoke to Solomon and said, "Solomon, my son, serve God and He will bless you." Then David showed Solomon the things he had got ready for building the house; gold and silver and iron and stones and wood and David asked the people whether they would give any of their things to build a house for God.

The people gave a great many things; gold and silver and bronze and iron and beautiful shiny stones and the people liked to give their things for God's house.

David was pleased to see that they liked to give; for that was a sign that they loved God.

If you love God you will like to spare your money to help poor people and to buy Bibles and to build churches and to send ministers to the heathen.

I shall tell you no more about David. I know that you like him very much. What a joy it is to love God all our lives long! This is what I wish you to do. I want you to lovc God now you are young and to go on loving Him when you are grown up, if you live and to love Him when your hair is grey. David began to sing God's praises when he was a shepherd boy and he went on praising Him till he died. God was kind to David all his days. He will be kind to you even when you are old and grey-headed and He will take you to that wonderful place where David is now and where Christ is.

Then David prayed to God and thanked Him for letting Solomon build Him a house and for letting the people give their things to God. And David asked God to make Solomon love Him and obey Him. David offered a great many sacrifices to God.

Afterwards all the people went to their own homes again and very soon David died.

Where did his spirit go? To the God he loved. He had sung many sweet songs to Him while he lived on the earth, but now he sings sweeter songs.

This was the name that was given to David: "The sweet Psalmist of Israel." Why do you think that name was given to him?

I shall now tell you about Solomon.

Questions for Chapter 28

What promise had God made to David long ago?
Which son was anointed king before David died?
What things did David give for building God's house?
Did anyone else give anything?
Why was David glad that the people liked to give their things to God?
What advice did David give to Solomon?
What name is given to David because he sang sweet psalms to God?
How long had David loved God?
What is the best time to begin to love God?

Scripture Verse

To love and praise the Lord all of one's life.
'I will sing unto the Lord as long as I live: I will sing praise to my God while I have my being.' - (Ps. 104:33).

* * * * * * * * * *

CHAPTER 29
SOLOMON AND THE WISE CHOICE

2 Chron.1:1-3. 1 Kings 3:3-15.

Almost the first thing that Solomon did, when he was made king, was to offer sacrifices to God.

He did not offer these sacrifices on Mount Zion, where the ark was, but he went to the place where the old tabernacle was, that Moses had made and where the great bronze altar was. There he offered a great many sacrifices to God. Why did he offer those sacrifices? To show that he loved God and wished to serve Him.

The night after Solomon had offered the sacrifices, God

spoke to Solomon while he was asleep and said, "Ask what I shall give you." You see God allowed Solomon to choose what he would like God to give him.

Do you not wish to know what Solomon chose to have?

What would you have asked for?

Now Solomon had just been made king and he saw what a hard thing it was to be a good king; for Solomon would judge the people. People who quarrelled with each other would come to Solomon and it is very hard, when people quarrel, to find out who is at fault and who ought to be punished.

Solomon wished to judge the people well and so he asked God to make him very wise.

God came to Solomon that night in a dream and Solomon said to God , "You have made me king over a great many people and I am very young and I do not know what I ought to do. Oh, make me very wise that I may judge the people well."

Did Solomon make a wise choice? Oh, yes, it was right in Solomon to wish to judge the people well.

God was very pleased with Solomon and He said, "You did not ask me to make you very rich, or make you live a long while, or make you conquer your enemies; but you asked for wisdom; therefore I will make you wiser than any man that ever lived and I will make you very rich too; so that no other king shall be as rich or as great as you and if you love me and serve me as David did, I will make you live a long while."

Then Solomon awoke. How pleased he must have been to think of the promise that God had made him! He went back to Jerusalem and offered up more sacrifices near the ark on Mount Zion.

Questions for Chapter 29

Where did Solomon first sacrifice to God?
What did God say to Solomon when he first spoke to him?
What did Solomon choose?
Why did Solomon wish for wisdom?
Was God pleased with Solomon's choice?
What did God promise him besides wisdom?
What kind of wisdom is better than Solomon's?
How can you get that best wisdom?

Scripture Verse

Where real wisdom begins.
'The fear of the Lord is the beginning of knowledge: but fools despise wisdom and instruction.' - (Prov. 1:7)

* * * * * * * * * *

CHAPTER 30
SOLOMON AND THE WISE JUDGMENT

1 Kings 3:16 to end.

Now I will tell you of something that happened which showed that God had made Solomon as wise as He said He would.

One day there came two women to Solomon. They had quarrelled with each other. Solomon was the judge and the women stood before him.

One of these women held a dead baby in her arms and the other held a living baby in her arms. Both the babies were very little creatures, only a few days old, so that the living baby was not old enough to sit up and to look about it, or to smile.

The woman who held the dead baby seemed very unhappy and she said to the king, "This dead baby is not my own baby, the other baby is mine. I lived in the same house with that woman and no one lived in the house besides us two. One night that woman lay upon her baby in her bed and killed it and so she got up and put her dead baby in my bed while I was asleep and took my living baby into hers. When I awoke in the morning I was going to feed my baby, but I found only this dead baby; but when I had looked at it, I saw it was not my own baby."

Then the other woman said, "You do not speak truth; the living baby is mine and the dead one is yours." Then the other woman said again, "No, the living baby is mine and the dead is yours."

Which of these women spoke the truth and which told lies? How could Solomon find out? How could he tell which ought to have the living baby? But God made Solomon very wise and he thought of a way to find out who spoke the truth.

Solomon called out, "Bring me a sword." And the servants brought a sword to the king. Then Solomon said, "Cut the living baby in two and give half to one woman and half to the other; because both the women say the child is theirs, so let them each have half."

Then one of the women cried out, "Oh, do not cut the child in half; but let that woman have it; only do not kill it."

But the other woman said, "Oh, let the child be cut in half and let us each have half."

Now which do you think was the mother of the living baby? Oh! I see that you know. Was it not the one who said, "Do not let it be killed?" How do you know that she was the mother? Because she loved the baby so much. Mothers would rather that anyone should have their babies than that the babies should be killed. Solomon knew which was the mother and he said to his servant, "Give her the living child and do not kill it; she is the mother of it."

Why had Solomon ordered the man at first to cut the baby in half? Had he intended to kill it? Oh, no! He only wanted to see what the women would say, that he might find out which was the mother. Was not that a wise plan of Solomon's? God had really made him as wise as He had promised He would.

All the Israelites heard of what the king had said to the women and they were surprised at his wisdom and they were afraid of him, for they saw that God had put wisdom into his heart.

Would you like to be wise? You come to school to learn to be wise, that you may know what is right and what is wrong; but you will never be as wise as Solomon, for God has said that no one shall be as wise as he was.

But there is one thing still better than Solomon's kind of wisdom and you may have it if you ask God for it. What is that? The Holy Spirit. If the Spirit is in your heart, you will know God and you will love Him. God has promised to give Him you. He has said, "Ask and ye shall have." I am glad when you are wise enough to answer questions right, or to behave well; but I wish most that you should love God in your heart and try to please Him. That is a better kind of wisdom than Solomon's.

Questions for Chapter 30

How did Solomon find out who was the mother of the living baby?

What did the mother of the living baby say when Solomon ordered that it should be cut in half?

How did saying that show that she was its mother?

Did Solomon intend that the baby should be cut in half?

Why then did he command the men to cut it in half?

Scripture Verse

Love given through the Holy Spirit.

'And hope maketh not ashamed; because the love of God is shed abroad in our hearts by the Holy Spirit which is given unto us.' - (Rom. 5:5).

* * * * * * * * * * *

CHAPTER 31

SOLOMON AND THE TEMPLE

1 Kings 5:15-17. 2 Chron. 3; 4; 5; 6; 7:1-12.

Do you remember what God had said that Solomon should build?

A house for the Lord.

This house would be called a temple and it would be very beautiful.

Solomon had a great many things to build it of; gold and silver, iron and bronze and stones and wood and he had a great many servants to build it. David, his father, had told him how to build it. How did David know how to build it? God had told David and he had written it down.

Solomon did not build the temple upon Mount Zion, but upon another high hill in Jerusalem.

Solomon ordered a great many large stones to be laid upon the ground for the beginning of the house; then he ordered his servants to cut down a great many trees. He had some more wood, which David had given to him. Solomon built the walls of wood and he put wood at the top and Solomon covered the inside of the house with gold.

How beautiful the house must have been inside! How bright it must have shone when the candlesticks were lighted; for Solomon made ten candlesticks of gold, to give light to the house. Solomon put other beautiful things in the temple, besides the ten candlesticks. He put ten tables for bread and a golden altar to burn sweet spices in the centre. And Solomon made a court round the temple; with a stone wall round the court and he put in the court ten large basins of bronze to wash the animals in before they were sacrificed and he made twelve oxen of bronze and put this large basin on the backs of the oxen and he had the basin filled with water for the priests to wash in.

In the court, Solomon placed a very large bronze altar that he had made. It was so large that a great many lambs, bullocks and goats might be burned on it at the same time.

At last the temple was quite finished and it was the most beautiful house in the world. It could not be moved about as the tabernacle had been in the wilderness; but Solomon never wished to move it from Jerusalem. It was a great deal larger than the tabernacle.

When it was finished, Solomon ordered all the people to come to the temple. The priests came and they carried the ark into a little room in the temple called the Holy of Holies. Solomon had made a great door to the little room and he had placed a great curtain or veil[1]) over the door and he had made two very large angels of wood, covered with gold and had placed them in the little room, besides the two golden angels that were on the top of the ark. The large angels stood upright and each had two great wings stretched out all across the little room; the priests left the ark under the wings of the great angels and no one could see into the little room because of the great door and of the curtain or veil which was over the door.

The other part of the temple was filled with priests and with singers all clothed in white and holding harps and other kinds of musical instruments in their hands - and some of the priests blew trumpets and these were the words the singers sang:-

"Oh, give thanks to the Lord; for he is good; for his mercy endures forever."

As soon as the priests had left the ark in the little room and while the priests and singers were praising the Lord in the temple, the Lord Himself came down in a cloud and filled the temple, so that the priests and singers were obliged to go out of the temple and stand in the court.

How glad Solomon was to see that the Lord had come into the house that he had buildt for Him! Solomon liked to see the brightness of the Lord, though he knew that the Lord filled every place.

Where did king Solomon stand? He had made a high place of bronze and he put it near the brazen altar in the court and he stood upon the high place, so that all the people could see him.

And Solomon knelt down on this place and spread wide his arms and began to pray to God. His prayer was very long; but I will only tell you a little part of it. He asked God to hear all people who were unhappy and who were sorry for their sins and to forgive them.

When Solomon had ended his prayer, there came down fire from heaven and burned up the beasts that had been killed and spread upon the altar. The fire did not hurt the people; it only burned the dead beasts on the altar. God sent the fire to show the people that he liked them to offer sacrifices to Him and to pray to Him.

When the people saw the fire and the glory of God all over the temple, they bowed themselves down to the ground and praised the Lord and said, "He is good; his mercy endures forever."

As last the people went home to their own houses, but they very often came to offer sacrifices at the temple and to pray to God. Sweet psalms and sweet music might be heard at the temple both night and day.

That temple was a delightful place; because there people praised God and because there they saw His glory.

There is a better place, where I hope we shall go some day. There God shines brighter than the sun and there angels clothed in white are always singing His praises. Would you like to go there? Then what must you do? You must pray to God for two things: to forgive you your sins and to give you His Holy Spirit. Why will God hear your prayers? Because Jesus died on the cross. God promised His Son that He would hear people's prayers. God cannot break His promise. Say to God, "Oh, keep Your promise to Your Son; forgive me for His sake; give me His Holy Spirit."

Questions for Chapter 31

Of what did Solomon build the temple?
What beautiful things did he put inside the temple?
What did he put in the court for the animals to be washed in?
What did he put in the Holy of Holies?
Why were the priests obliged to get out of the temple, just after they had put the ark in the Holy of Holies?
Who prayed aloud before all the people?
What did Solomon pray to God to do?
How did God show that He was pleased with Solomon's sacrifices?
What used to be heard in the temple night and day?
Why is heaven like a temple?
If you wish to go there, what must you pray God to give you?
Why does God hear people's prayers?

Scripture Verse

Repentance and the promise of the Holy Spirit.

'Then Peter said unto them, "Repent and be baptized every

one of you in the name of Jesus Christ for the remission of sins and ye shall receive the gift of the Holy Spirit."' - (Acts 2:38).

Notes for Chapter 31

1. Compare 1 Kings 6:31 with 2 Chron. 3:14.

* * * * * * * * * *

CHAPTER 32
SOLOMON AND THE QUEEN'S VISIT

2 Chron.7:11 to end. 1 Kings 10.

You remember how God once spoke to Solomon in the night and how He let him choose what he would have.

A long while afterwards God spoke to Solomon again in the night.

God said to Solomon, "I have heard your prayer and I will hear the people who pray to me in the temple and if you will obey me as David did, I will bless you; but if you do wicked things and worship idols, then I shall be very angry and this beautiful house that you have built shall be thrown down."

Ah! do you not hope that Solomon will obey God? How kind God had been to him! Had He not given him all the things He had promised?

Solomon was very rich and very wise, as God had promised. He built a great many ships and he built a palace and he built a great many towns. He made a great throne with six steps all covered with gold and images of two lions on each of the steps, a lion on each side and a seat at the top for Solomon.

When Solomon spoke, he said such wise things that people came from a great way off to hear him talk and they brought him presents; some brought cups of gold or silver and some brought him clothes and some brought spices and some brought horses and mules.

So Solomon grew very rich indeed. He sent his ships to far countries over the sea and they came back full of gold and silver and ivory and apes and peacocks. Solomon was the richest king in all the world.

I told you that people came from far countries to hear him say wise things; for Solomon knew a great deal; he knew about all the plants, from the highest tree down to the least plant that grows; he knew about the beasts and birds and fishes and worms and insects; but he knew something much better than these things - he knew about God and how to please Him and he gave people very wise advice.

Now there was a queen who lived a great way off, who heard of Solomon and of how wise he was and she wished very much to hear him talk and to see the house that he had built.

She had a great many questions to ask him; I believe that her questions were about God. She had not been taught about God in her own country and she wanted to know a great deal about Him. She was called the Queen of Sheba. It was right of the Queen of Sheba to want to know about God. She was a very rich lady, so she brought a great many servants with her and a great many camels with spices and gold, as presents to king Solomon.

Solomon was very kind to her and answered all the questions that she asked him and he showed her all the things that he had built. The queen was surprised at all she saw and heard and she said to king Solomon, "How happy are your servants who are always standing near you and who hear the wise things you say! Blessed be the Lord your God, who made you king."

Then she gave a great deal of gold and silver to king Solomon and he gave her all the things that she liked to have and then the queen went back with her camels and her servants into her own country.

The Queen of Sheba brought back to her home something

better than her presents; she brought a great deal of wisdom in her mind from the wise things Solomon said. I hope that she left off worshipping idols and loved the true God.

A great many of the wise things that Solomon said are written down in the Bible; they are called "The Proverbs." When you are older you shall read them, so that you may grow wise. I think even now you would understand some of them. I think that the Queen of Sheba would think you very happy children if she could see you. Are you not happier than Solomon's servants? You can read the wise things that Solomon said and a great many wiser things that Jesus Christ said. They are written down in the Bible.

Questions for Chapter 32

What did God say to Solomon when He spoke to him the second time in the night?
Why did the people come to Solomon from a great way off?
How did Solomon grow very rich?
What things did Solomon know about?
Which queen came to hear Solomon?
Why did she think Solomon's servants happy?
What were the wise things that Solomon said called?
Where are they written down?
Why are you happier than Solomon's servants?

Scripture Verse

The authority and wisdom of Jesus' teaching.
'And when he was come into his own country, he taught them in their synagogue, insomuch that they were astonished and said, Whence hath this man this wisdom and these mighty works?' - (Matt. 13:54).

CHAPTER 33
SOLOMON AND THE IDOLS

1 Kings 11:1-13.

How many times had God appeared to Solomon? Twice. The first time God promised to make Solomon wise and the next time God promised to bless him, if he served Him.

But did Solomon serve God? I must now tell you of the wicked things that he did when he was old.

He married a great many wives. This was wrong. In those times people might have two wives or more; but God liked best that they should only have one. You remember that Jacob had two wives, named Rachel and Leah. If a man *now* was to have two wives, he would be punished; *then* he might have two wives; but not so many as Solomon had.

Solomon had seven hundred wives. Why did he have so many? I think that Solomon had grown proud and that he wished to be a very grand king and that it was thought very grand for a king to have many wives.

These wives were wicked; they worshipped idols. Solomon should not have married heathen women. At last these wives persuaded Solomon to like their idols and to build altars for the idols on the high places round Jerusalem and Solomon did even worse than this; he worshipped some of the idols himself. You did not think that he could have been so wicked. Was he not very foolish to worship idols, which are only made of wood or stone? Solomon knew what was right, but he did not do it.

How sad it must have been to see these women offering sacrifices and burning incense to their idols and Solomon bowing down to them! God was very angry with Solomon and God said to him, "Because you have done this, one of your servants shall make himself king; he shall take away a great deal of the land of Canaan from your son, as soon as you are dead."

I believe Solomon was sorry for his wickedness before he died; but I am not quite sure that he was. It must have made him very sorry to know that God would punish him! I hope he was sorry for having displeased God, who had been so very kind to him.

Do you know it is the rule that when a king dies the king's son is king instead of his father? So when Solomon died, his son was king instead of him; but very soon one of Solomon's servants tried to make himself king. The servant's name was Jer-o-bo-am. This servant made himself the king over a great part of the land of Canaan; but Solomon's son was still king over the rest of the land.

What God had said came true; for God makes all he says come true. God had told Solomon that his son should only have part of the land. This was the punishment that God gave Solomon. God will punish people who are disobedient.

I hope that you will not be like king Solomon and love God only when you are young. I hope that you will love God all your life, from the time you are young until your hair is grey and your back is bent with age, should you live to be old.

Questions for Chapter 33

What sort of wives did Solomon marry? How many?
Why did Solomon worship idols in his old age?
What did he do for the idols?
What punishment did God give to Solomon?
Was Solomon's son king over part of the land of Canaan?
Who made himself king over the other part of Canaan?

Scripture Verse

To love and praise the Lord all of one's life.
'I will sing unto the Lord as long as I live: I will sing praise to my God while I have my being.' - (Ps. 104:33).

* * * * * * * * * * *

CHAPTER 34
JEROBOAM AND THE DRIED-UP HAND

1 Kings 12:25 to end; 13:1-10, 33,34.

You have heard how Solomon's servant, Jeroboam, made himself king over part of Canaan; but Solomon's son was king over the other part of Canaan. Now Jerusalem was not in Jeroboam's part of Canaan; it was in the part that Solomon's son was king over. It was a good thing for Solomon's son that he had Jerusalem. You can tell me why it was a good thing. The temple was in Jerusalem and in the temple God came down in a glorious cloud.

You know that God had commanded all the people in Canaan to come to Jerusalem very often to worship Him. Jeroboam ought to have come to Jerusalem to worship God; but he would not. He was very wicked and he told his people not to go to Jerusalem.

Why did he not like to go there? Because there was another king in Jerusalem. He did not like his people to go to a place where there was another king, in case they should like the other king best. You see how proud Jeroboam was. Then Jeroboam did a very wicked thing; he made two golden calves and set them up in his part of Canaan, one calf in one town and the other calf in another town. Why did he set up the calves? That people might worship them instead of God. He told his people to worship them. He said, "Do not go to Jerusalem, it is too far off; worship these golden calves." How wicked it was of Jeroboam to teach his people to worship idols! It is very wicked to teach other people to do wrong. Remember this; never advise your playfellows to do wrong. God will be very angry with you if you do and you will be like the devil; for he tempts people to sin against God.

Jeroboam worshipped the calves himself. One day God sent a prophet to him, to tell him of his wickedness. Jeroboam was standing by an altar burning incense to a golden calf, when the prophet came and told him how angry God was with the people who worshipped the golden calves and how he would punish them. And the prophet said, "And this is the sign that God is angry: the altar shall be broken and the ashes that are on it shall fall to the ground."

When king Jeroboam heard this he was angry and he wished to punish the prophet; so he stretched out his hand and said to his servants, "Lay hold on him." Now while Jeroboam's hand was stretched out, God made it grow dry and stiff, so that he could not pull it back again and at the same time the altar was broken and the ashes fell upon the ground, as the prophet had said.

Do you not think Jeroboam must have been frightened then? He knew that no one could make his hand well but God; so he said to the prophet, "Pray to the Lord your God for me, that my hand may be made well."

Would the prophet pray to God for Jeroboam, who had been so unkind to him? Yes, he would; he prayed to God and God made the king's hand as well as it was before.

Then Jeroboam did not try to hurt the prophet any more, because he was afraid of hurting him; but Jeroboam did not repent of worshipping idols and turn to God, but he went on teaching his people to pray to the golden calves. And God was very angry with Jeroboam.

Why was not Jeroboam afraid of God? He saw that God could dry up his arm; could He not kill him and cast him into hell? Ah! We ought to fear to offend our great God. Have you never stretched out your arm to do something naughty? To fight? God could have dried up your arm. He is very kind. But He will punish us one day, if we do not love Him, or care for him.

Questions for Chapter 34

Was Jeroboam king over all the land of Canaan?
Who was king over the other part?
Was Jerusalem in Jeroboam's part of the land?
Why ought Jeroboam to have come very often to Jerusalem?
Why did he advise his people not to go to Jerusalem?
What wicked thing did Jeroboam teach his people to do?
Why did God send a prophet to Jeroboam?
Why did God make Jeroboam's hand stiff and dry?
Who prayed to God to make it well again?
Did Jeroboam repent of his wickedness?
Does God always dry up people's hands, when they are stretched out to do wrong?

Scripture Verse

A healthy fear of the Lord is the wise way.
'The fear of the Lord *is* the beginning of knowledge: *but* fools despise wisdom and instruction.' - (Prov. 1:7)

CHAPTER 35
ELIJAH AND THE RAVENS

1 Kings 16:29 to end; 17:1-7.

You remember that Jeroboam was king over only part of the land of Canaan. Solomon had been king over all the land; but now Solomon's son was king over one part and Jeroboam was king over the other part.

I will tell you what Jeroboam was called. He was called King of Israel and Solomon's son, Rehoboam, was called King of Judah. Will you try to remember this?

At last Jeroboam died and there was another king of Israel instead of him and at last the king died and then there was another king and at last he died and then there was another king; so there were a great many kings one after the other. I am sorry to say that they were all wicked and that they all worshipped the golden calves that Jeroboam had made.

At last, after a great many kings had died, one after another, there was a king called Ahab.

He was more wicked than any of the other kings had been. One of the worst things he did was to marry a woman who worshipped idols. This woman was the daughter of the king of another country, called Sidon. She had been brought up to worship idols; she was very fond of them and she did a great many wicked things. This woman's name was Jezebel. She was called the Queen of Israel, because she was married to Ahab, king of Israel.

The name of Jezebel's favourite idol was Baal and she persuaded Ahab to worship Baal, as well as the golden calves and Ahab built a temple for Baal in the town where he lived. There were a great many men who used to teach people to worship Baal and these men were called prophets of Baal and Jezebel was very kind to them. For Jezebel was kind to people who loved idols, but she tried to kill the people who loved God. There were some people in the land of Israel who would not worship Baal and these people hid themselves in caves to avoid Jezebel. God loved these poor people very much.

I will now tell you of one very good prophet that lived in the land of Israel. His name was Elijah; he would not worship idols and he tried to persuade other people to love the true God. God often spoke to him and told him what would happen and Elijah prayed very often to God.

Ahab and Jezebel hated Elijah because he was good and they would have liked to kill him. Elijah was very sorry to see so many people in the land of Israel worshipping Baal and he wished very much that they should be sorry for their wickedness. At last God sent the people a punishment.

God sent no rain for a great many months, nor did he let any dew come down on the grass in the morning; so the hot sun scorched the grass and the corn did not grow and the trees did not produce fruit. All the people of Israel were very unhappy; but God wished them to turn from their wickedness.

How did Elijah get food when there was no rain? God told him to go to a place where there was a pond or brook, in a secret place, where he might hide himself from Ahab and God promised to send some ravens to feed him.

So Elijah went to this brook and he drank water from the brook. Every morning some ravens flew to him and gave him some bread and meat and every evening they came again and brought him some more bread and meat. The next day they came again, both morning and evening; so Elijah had breakfast and supper every day and he wanted nothing more.

Who made the birds so wise and so kind? God can do

everything. Most ravens are fierce, but God made these ravens gentle. How glad Elijah must have been when he saw them coming with the food! How he must have thanked God for sending them every day! God has promised to feed all hungry people who pray to Him. God does not send ravens to feed them; but He makes other people pity them and give them food.

Elijah lived quite alone by the brook; but Elijah knew that God was with him. At last there was very little water in the brook; the sun dried up the water and no rain came to fill it up. There was less water every day and at last there was none left.

What could Elijah do now? God could have filled the brook with water, but he did not choose to do that. He told Elijah to leave the brook and go to another place.

I will tell you soon where Elijah went.

You see what care God took of Elijah; he will take the same care of you, if you love Him and pray to Him.

Questions for Chapter 35

Was Jeroboam called king of Israel or king of Judah?
Who was called king of Judah?
When Jeroboam died, was there another king of Israel?
Were there a great many kings of Israel, who lived one after the other?
Were they good or wicked?
Who was Ahab?
What was the name of his wife?
What was the name of her favourite idol?
What sort of people did Jezebel try to kill?
What punishment did God send to the people of Israel for worshipping idols?
Which prophet was fed by ravens?

Why did Elijah leave the place where the ravens fed him?

Scripture Verse

Look to God for help.
'I will lift up mine eyes unto the hills, from whence cometh my help. My help cometh from the Lord, which made heaven and earth.' - (Ps. 121:1,2).

* * * * * * * * * *

CHAPTER 36
ELIJAH AND THE WIDOW

1 Kings 17:8 to end.

Where did God tell Elijah to go when the brook dried up? He told him to go a great way off to a place where a poor widow lived, who would give him food. You know that a widow is a woman who has lost her husband. Widows are generally poor, because they have no husbands to work for them and this widow was very poor indeed, because, since there had been no rain, people could get very little food to eat, because so little corn grew in the fields.

But Elijah went where God told him. He went all across the land of Canaan, till he came to Zarephath, just outside Canaan. Now the people who lived in this town were heathen people and worshipped idols.

When Elijah came to the gate of the town, he saw a poor woman gathering sticks and Elijah saw that she was the widow who was to give him food and Elijah called to her and said, "Fetch me, I pray, a little water in a cup, that I may drink."

I do not wonder that Elijah was thirsty, for he had walked a long way and there was now very little water in the land of Canaan.

Now this widow was so kind that she went to fetch the water for Elijah. Then Elijah called to her again and said, "Bring me, I pray, a piece of bread in your hand."

The poor widow said, "I have not got any bread; I have only a handful of flour in a barrel and a little oil in a jar and I was just gathering some sticks, that I might make a fire and make the flour and oil into a little cake, that I and my son may eat it and as we have no more food, when we have eaten it we must die."

Would Elijah take all the poor widow's food? God had told Elijah what to say.

Elijah said to the widow, "Go and make a little cake for me first and afterwards make one for you and your son; for God has said that there shall always be some flour in your barrel and some oil in your jar, till He sends rain again upon the earth."

What a wonderful promise this was! Did the widow believe it? Yes, she did. She went and made a fire and mixed the flour and oil together and made some bread for Elijah and then she made some for herself and her son and still there was flour in the barrel and oil in the jar and every day she found enough flour and oil to make bread for them all.

Elijah came and lodged with this poor widow; he lived in a room upstairs near her house. The widow found it was a good thing to have such a man as Elijah in the house. Why was it such a good thing? Because God made the flour and oil last. Besides this, Elijah could teach this poor woman about God; for you know that she had been brought up to worship idols.

Elijah loved God and wished all people to love Him.

Now you shall hear of a very sad thing that happened to this poor woman. One day her son, who was a little boy, fell sick and he was so very sick that he died and there was no breath left in him. The poor widow was very unhappy. She knew that God had let him die and she thought that God was angry with her. She wished that Elijah had not come to her house and went and spoke angrily to him. It was very ungrateful of her to behave in this manner. Then Elijah said, "Give me your son."

Now the widow was holding the dead child in her arms and Elijah took the child in his own arms and carried him to his own room and laid him on his bed. Then Elijah began to pray to God. "Oh, Lord my God," he said, "have You made this sad thing happen to the widow I live with? Have You killed her son?"

Then Elijah stretched himself upon the child as it lay dead; he did so three times and he prayed to God, saying, "Oh, Lord, my God, I pray, let this child's soul come into him again."

And the Lord heard Elijah's prayer and He let the child's soul come into him again and then the child came back to life. Then he was warm and he breathed. Oh, how glad Elijah must have been! How kind it was of God to hear Elijah's prayer! God let the poor widow know that Elijah's God was the true God and could make people alive. Elijah took the child in his arms and brought him downstairs and gave him to his mother again and said to her, "See, your son is alive."

Was she now angry with Elijah? Oh, no. "Now," said she, "I see that you are a man of God and that all you tell me about God is true."

Now, I hope the widow believed all that Elijah said and I hope she loved the God who had been so very kind to her and given her food and made her child alive again.

God still hears people when they pray; but He does not always make children alive again; but He will make you alive again when the last trumpet sounds, if you love him. Some day your body will lie in the ground and then I hope your soul will be with God and when Christ comes in the clouds and the trumpet sounds, then your body will rise from the grave and your soul and body will be joined together again. Oh, what a happy day that will be!

Questions for Chapter 36

Was the widow who fed Elijah a heathen or an Israelite?
What food had she in her house?
What promise did Elijah make to her, if she would feed him?
Did the woman believe this promise?
Why was the widow angry with Elijah?
How did Elijah show the widow that his God was the true God?
When will dead people be made to live again?

Scripture Verse

Jesus will come for those who love him.

'For the Lord himself shall descend from heaven with a shout, ... and the dead in Christ shall rise first: Then we which are alive *and* remain shall be caught up together with them in the clouds, to meet the Lord in the air: and so shall we ever be with the Lord.' - (1 Thess. 4:16,17).

* * * * * * * * * *

CHAPTER 37

ELIJAH AND THE SURPRISE

1 Kings. 18:1 - 20.

Elijah lived a long time with the poor widow. Ahab and Jezebel, the wicked king and queen, did not know where he was hiding. They would have been glad to find him and kill him. Ahab sent to all the countries around to look for him, but no one could find him. Why was king Ahab angry with Elijah?

Because Elijah had told Ahab that God was angry with him for worshipping idols. You know that wicked people once hated Jesus, because He told them of their sins.

The Israelites were very unhappy, because they had very little food; even king Ahab did not have enough grass in his fields for his horses, so that a great many of them died.

Elijah was sorry for the poor Israelites and he prayed to God[1] to send rain, that more corn and grass might grow. God heard this prayer and he told Elijah that He would soon send rain; but first He told Elijah to go and show himself to king Ahab.

Do you not think that Elijah would be afraid to go to king Ahab? But Elijah did what God told him; for he knew that God could take care of him. So Elijah left the poor widow and her son and set out on a long journey to the place where Ahab lived. I think that the widow must have been sorry when Elijah went, for he had fed her and taught her about God; but God had promised to make her flour and oil last till He sent rain and the rain had not come yet.

Now while Elijah was on his way to king Ahab, he met a very good servant of Ahab's. The servant's name was Obadiah. This servant was looking for some grass for king Ahab's horses. Obadiah knew Elijah when he saw him and he was very surprised, for it was a long while since anyone in Canaan had seen Elijah. This good servant fell on his face before Elijah and said, "Are you my Lord Elijah?"

Then Elijah said, "I am; go and tell your Lord (King Ahab) that I am here."

Then Obadiah was afraid, for he thought that while he was away telling Ahab where Elijah was, God would take away Elijah to some other place and then that Ahab would be angry with his servant and kill him. Ahab was a cruel master and his servant was afraid of making him angry.

But Elijah promised that he would stay in that place till King

Ahab had come; so the servant believed Elijah's promise and went to look for king Ahab.

Ahab was in another place, looking for grass for his horses. His good servant told him that Elijah was waiting to see him. So Ahab came to the place.

When Ahab saw Elijah, he spoke angrily to him and he said, "Are you the man that troubles the people of Israel?"

Ahab thought it was Elijah who had asked God not to let the rain come.

Then Elijah said to Ahab, "It is not I that trouble the people of Israel; it is you who has made these troubles come by your wickedness. You have not obeyed God and you have worshipped Baal."

Then Elijah told Ahab what he wanted him to do. He told him to get all the prophets of Baal together and send them to him to a very high hill or mountain.

Would Ahab do what Elijah asked him? Yes, he would, because he wanted rain and he thought that Elijah would ask God to send it. I think that Ahab was afraid of killing Elijah, in case God should send no rain.

Questions for Chapter 37

Why did Elijah leave the poor widow at last?
Whom did Elijah meet on his way to King Ahab?
What command did Elijah give to the servant?
Why was the servant afraid to tell Ahab that he had found Elijah?
What was Ahab doing when the servant called him?
Did Ahab kill Elijah when he saw him?
What did he say to Elijah?
What did Elijah ask Ahab to do?

Scripture Verse

God even blesses the unbeliever with sun and rain.
'...for he maketh his sun to rise on the evil and on the good and sendeth rain on the just and on the unjust.' - (Matt. 5:45).

Notes for Chapter 37

1. James 5:18.

* * * * * * * * * *

CHAPTER 38
ELIJAH AND THE TWO ALTARS

1 Kings 18:20-40.

One morning Elijah was on the high mountain with Baal's wicked prophets and a great many people were standing all round and King Ahab was there, but Jezebel was not there.

What could Elijah have to say to the people?

He wanted them to see that his God was the true God; so Elijah said to them, "Let Baal's prophets take a bullock and kill it and lay it on an altar and then let them ask Baal to send fire from heaven to burn up the bullock. I will take another bullock and kill it and lay it on the altar and I will ask the Lord to send fire from heaven and if Baal sends fire, then you will know that he is the true God; but if my God sends fire, then you will know that He is the true God."

The people liked what Elijah said and they answered, "It is well spoken."

Then Elijah told Baal's prophets to take their bullock first. So they took it and killed it and put it on an altar with some wood; but they put no fire to the wood. Then they began to pray to their god to send fire. They cried, "Oh, Baal, hear us!"

till twelve o'clock and they jumped about the altar, as they used to do when they prayed to him.

How tired they must have been after calling out so long, "Oh, Baal, hear us!"

At last Elijah said to them, "Cry louder. Perhaps your god is talking, or perhaps he is hunting, or perhaps he is taking a journey, or perhaps he is asleep and you must awake him."

Was Elijah speaking in earnest? Oh no, he knew that Baal was nothing at all; only those foolish people said that there was a god called Baal and worshipped images that they said were like him.

Still the prophets of Baal went on praying for fire and at last they cut themselves with knives and made their blood flow, because they thought it would please Baal; they thought he was a cruel god that liked blood. So they went on till three o'clock in the afternoon; but no fire came from heaven.

Then Elijah said it was time to ask his God to send fire; so Elijah built an altar with twelve stones and hc laid some wood on the altar and he laid a bullock on the altar and then he instructed the people to throw twelve barrels of water over the altar. There was a river just at the bottom of the hill and a well also, where people could fetch the water; Elijah made a ditch all round the altar and this ditch was quite filled with water and the altar was quite wet.

Why did Elijah command the water to be poured over the sacrifice? To show the people that he had not hidden any fire in the altar, nor near it; for if he had, the water would have put it out.

Then Elijah began to pray to God. All the people were standing round, while he prayed before the altar.

This is what he said, "Lord God of Abraham, of Isaac and

of Israel (or Jacob), let it be known this day that you are God and that I am Your servant. Hear me, Oh, Lord, hear me."

Did God hear Elijah? Yes; the fire came from heaven and burnt up the bullock and the altar; yes, the fire burnt the stones and even the water that was in the ditch.

How surprised the people were at this sight! They fell on their faces and said, "The Lord he is the God; the Lord he is the God."

Now they saw that Baal was not the true God. So Elijah instructed the people to take hold of the wicked prophets of Baal and to bring them down to the river at the bottom of the hill and to kill them with swords. So the blood of these prophets was mixed with the water in the river. These prophets had taught the people to worship Baal, so God chose that they should die.

Did the people leave off worshipping Baal? Did they listen to what Elijah said and pray to his God? We shall soon hear what they did.

How they wished that God would send rain! They must have felt sure that if God could send fire, He could send rain.

He sends down rain to make corn grow for us does He not? Oh, what a great God He is!

He could send fire to burn us, but instead of that He is kind to us.

Questions for Chapter 38

Why did Elijah wish all these people to come to the mountain?
Who prayed first - Elijah or the people?
What did the people say to Baal?
Why did not Baal send fire?
How did Elijah laugh at them?
Why did Elijah pour water over the altar he had built?

What was Elijah's prayer?
What did the people cry out when the fire came down?
Why did Elijah command the prophets of Baal to be killed?

Scripture Verse

God commands His people to worship Him alone.
'I am the Lord thy God, which have brought thee out of the land of Egypt, out of the house of bondage. Thou shalt have no other gods before me.' - (Ex. 20:2,3).

* * * * * * * * * *

CHAPTER 39
ELIJAH AND THE RAIN

1 Kings 18:41 to end; 19:1-3.

You have heard how the prophets of Baal were killed. Now Elijah knew that God would soon send rain; so he told Ahab that there would soon be rain and that he might go and eat and drink. So Ahab ate and drank in some place near the high hill. But Elijah did not eat and drink. He went up to the top of the hill to pray to God. He threw himself down upon the earth and bent down his head very low.

Elijah had a servant. You have never heard of his servant before and I do not know who he was.

Elijah told his servant to stand up while he himself was praying and to look a great way off over the sea and to tell him what he saw. Do you know what Elijah wished his servant to see? What is it that comes before rain - those dark things in the sky? Clouds. Elijah wanted God to send clouds into the sky, that there might be rain. The servant went up and looked and then said to Elijah, "There is nothing." Then Elijah told him to go and look seven times. The seventh time the servant came and told Elijah, "I saw a little cloud a great way off, as big as a man's hand."

Elijah knew that God had heard his prayer and that the cloud would grow larger and that rain would soon be poured down. So he told the servant to tell Ahab to get ready his chariot and his horses and to drive as fast as he could to his own house, which was a great way off, for there would soon be a great deal of rain.

So Ahab rode in his chariot with his horses and God made Elijah so strong that he ran faster than the horses and he got first to the city where Ahab lived. While Ahab was driving and Elijah was running, there were a great many clouds in the sky and soon there was a great rain.

How glad the people were when the rain came down! It filled the dried-up ponds and refreshed the withered grass and softened the hard ground. Now the people knew that more corn and grass would soon grow in the fields. It was kind of God to send the rain. Ought not the people to love God, who sent the rain, though they had been so wicked as to worship Baal?

Shouldn't we love God, who sends us rain so often and makes the corn grow? We are naughty and do not deserve to have rain.

When Ahab got to his own city where he lived, he found the queen Jezebel there and he told her all that had happened; he told her how Baal did not send fire from heaven and how God did and he told her how Elijah had killed the prophets of Baal.

Shouldn't Jezebel have said that she would worship the God who sent fire from heaven? But she did not say this; she was very angry with Elijah and she sent a man to tell him that she would kill him the next day.

I think she was afraid of Elijah, or she would have ordered the man to kill him that same day; but perhaps she thought, if she killed Elijah, there would be no more rain.

When Elijah heard that Jezebel wished to kill him, he was afraid and he would not stay in the city where she lived, but he went very quickly all through the land of Canaan, till he came to a great wilderness. He did not take his servant with him, but he went there alone. In the wilderness there were trees and hills, but very few houses and people.

Elijah was quite alone in the wilderness. At last he sat down under a tree and he prayed to God to let him die. Why was Elijah so unhappy? Was it because he was afraid of Jezebel killing him? He was more unhappy because Jezebel went on in her wickedness. Elijah saw that she would go on teaching people to worship idols and he wished everybody to love God. After Elijah had prayed, he lay down under the tree and he went to sleep. Soon someone touched him. Who was it? An angel. The angel said, "Arise and eat."

Then Elijah looked and saw a fire and some bread near it, that had been just baked and he saw a jug of water close to his head. Who could have got ready the bread and the water for Elijah? It must have been the angel. So you see that an angel was his servant. God sends His angels to wait upon people who love Him. The angels like to wait upon them; they fly down quickly from heaven when God tells them. Yes the angels take care of you.

Elijah ate and drank the bread and water and then he lay down again and slept. But soon the angel woke him again and said, "Arise and eat, for you will soon walk a great way."

So Elijah ate and drank again and afterwards Elijah walked a great way in the wilderness; but the angel's food had made him strong and he lived without eating and drinking for forty days. Was not that a great wonder? God can keep people alive without food, if He chooses to do so. Did He not keep the Lord Jesus alive for forty days without food?

You see how kind God was to Elijah, when he was unhappy. I have often advised you to pray to God when you are unhappy, because I know that He can comfort you.

If you are sick, pray to God; He can make you well. If you are in disgrace, pray to Him; He can make you good. If you are alone and frightened, pray to Him; He can keep you safely.

Questions for Chapter 39

Why did Elijah go to the top of a mountain, while Ahab was eating and drinking?
Why did Elijah command his servant to watch?
What did the servant see at last?
Where did Elijah tell Ahab to go before it began to rain?
Who ran before Ahab's chariot?
Who told Jezebel what had happened?
What *ought* Jezebel to have done when she heard that Elijah's God had sent fire from heaven?
What message did she send to Elijah?
Where did he go?
Why was he very unhappy?
Whom did God send to feed him?
Do angels still wait upon people who love God?
How many days did Elijah live without food?

Scripture Verse

Do not fear, rather come to God in prayer.

'Be careful for nothing; but in every thing by prayer and supplication with thanksgiving let your requests be made known unto God. And the peace of God, which passeth all understanding, shall keep your hearts and minds through Christ Jesus.' - (Phil. 4:6,7).

* * * * * * * * * *

CHAPTER 40
ELIJAH AND THE CALL OF ELISHA

1 Kings 19 to end.

Elijah walked for forty days in the wilderness quite alone, till at last he came to a mountain. There he found a cave and he went into the cave and slept in it. While he was in the cave, God spoke to him and asked him why he had come there.

You know the reason why. You know that Elijah had left Canaan because of the wicked Jezebel and God knew this; but He chose Elijah to tell Him why.

Then Elijah said, "The people of Israel have thrown down God's altars and killed God's prophets and I am the only one left and they try to kill me."

Then God told him to come out of the cave. Then Elijah came out and stood upon the mountain. And God made a very great wind blow, that tore the mountain; then God made the mountain shake and then God made a fire come. How dreadful it must have been to see and hear these things! But God wanted to show Elijah how strong He was; so that Elijah might know that God could take care of him and could punish the wicked people who tried to hurt him. Then God spoke to Elijah in a very gentle voice and when Elijah heard this voice, he covered his face with his cloak and went and stood inside the cave.

It was kind of God to speak to Elijah in such a gentle voice! God loved Elijah and wished to comfort him. But Elijah remembered what a great God He was; so he hid his face. The angels, who stand round God's throne in heaven, hide their faces between their wings.[1] Shouldn't all people fear the Lord? When you pray to God, do you remember what a great God He is? How can children be so bold as to look about and play at prayer-time?

God asked Elijah again why he came there and then Elijah told the Lord again, that the people were wicked and that they wanted to kill him.

Then God told Elijah that He would soon punish the wicked people for worshipping idols and God said that *all* the people did not worship Baal and that there were a great many in Israel who had never bowed their knees to Baal, nor kissed his image with their mouths.

Elijah thought that no one loved God but himself. How glad he must have been when he heard there were many other people besides who loved God! God knows who loves Him and who does not. He counts them and remembers them.[2]

God told Elijah to go and find a man called Elisha and to anoint him to be a prophet.

Would not Elijah be pleased that there should be another prophet to teach people about God?

Then Elijah left the cave and he went to look for Elisha. At last he came to a field where a man was ploughing. There were twenty-four oxen drawing the plough. They were harnessed two and two and each two had a great piece of wood over their necks, called a yoke. A man was walking by the side of the two last of the oxen. The man's name was Elisha.

Elijah came up to the man and taking off his own cloak, threw it over the man's shoulders. Why did he throw the cloak over the man? He wished to show him that he was to come with him. The man knew what Elijah meant so he left his oxen and ran after Elijah and said, "I will come with you; only let me first go and kiss my father and mother."

It was right of Elisha to be ready to go with Elijah; because Elijah was a prophet of the Lord's. I do not wonder the man wished to go first to take leave of his father and mother and his friends. Would you not wish to take leave of your parents, if you were going away from them?

Elijah allowed the man to go home for a little while. When the man went home he made a feast for all his friends. He killed two of his oxen and he made a fire with the wood that was upon their necks and roasted them and then asked his friends to come and eat their meat.

Then he left his home and went after Elijah and he was Elijah's servant. It was very right of the man to go with Elijah. Do you think it would be pleasant to live with Elijah? Yes; it would be pleasant to hear Elijah talk of God and to hear him preach and pray. But you know that wicked people hated Elijah and so Elijah was often obliged to hide himself. If this man had not loved God, he would have liked to stay at home with his friends better than being with Elijah. But he did love God - God loved him and blessed him. How pleasant it is to obey God! Being with parents and friends cannot make us so happy as knowing that we please God.

Questions for Chapter 40

After Elijah had walked forty days through the wilderness where did he come at last?

What terrible things did he hear and see in the cave?

What was it Elijah did when he heard God's gentle voice?

Why had Elijah left the land of Canaan?

Were there any people in Canaan who had not worshipped Baal?

Whom was Elijah to anoint to be prophet?

What did he find Elisha doing?

Why did Elijah throw his cloak over Elisha?
What did Elisha wish to do before he went with Elijah?
If Elisha had been a wicked man, would he have liked to go with Elijah?
Why not?

Scripture Verse

Jesus like our great shepherd calls us to go and follow him. 'My sheep hear my voice and I know them and they follow me.' - (John 10:27).

Notes for Chapter 40

1. Isa. 6:2. 2. 2 Tim. 2:19.

* * * * * * * * * *

CHAPTER 41
ELIJAH AND NABOTH'S VINEYARD

1 Kings 21.

I am going to tell you of a very wicked thing that Ahab did. People who worship idols always do a great many other wicked things; but people who love God, hate lying and stealing and all wicked things.

Ahab was very rich. He had two houses. One of his houses was in another town a good way off. Near one of these houses there was a garden full of vines. What fruit grows on the vine? Grapes. A garden of vines is called a vineyard. This vineyard was close to Ahab's house and belonged to a man named Naboth. Ahab wished very much to have this vineyard that he might make it into a garden for himself. So Ahab said to Naboth, "If you will give me your vineyard I will give you a better one instead, or I will give you some money for it."

But Naboth answered, "No, I will not sell my vineyard; my father gave it to me and I do not choose to sell it."

Was it wrong of Naboth not to sell his vineyard? No, it was not wrong; he might keep it if he pleased.

But Ahab was very angry, because he could not get the vineyard and he went home to his other house. There he was so unhappy that he lay down upon his bed and turned away his face and would not eat any bread.

How foolish Ahab was to be unhappy about a vineyard! He had a great many beautiful things, yet he wanted more. But people who do not love God always want more things and are never satisfied.

Now Jezebel saw how unhappy Ahab seemed and she went to him and said, "What makes you so sad? Why do you not eat?"

And Ahab said, "I asked Naboth to sell me his vineyard and he said, 'I will not sell it.'"

Then Jezebel said, "Are you not a king? Do not be unhappy; eat and drink; I will give you the vineyard."

How could Jezebel get the vineyard? Oh! She had such a wicked plan in her mind - she meant to have Naboth killed. So she wrote some letters to some wicked judges who lived near Naboth and she told them to instruct some other wicked people to say that they had heard Naboth say very wicked words against God and the king and then to order people to kill him.

Then Jezebel sent those wicked letters to the judges in the town where Naboth lived. When they had read them, they did as she told them. They instructed two men to say that they had heard Naboth say very wicked words against God and the king. Then the judges said that Naboth must be killed and the people took him out of the city and threw stones at him till he died. Poor Naboth's blood flowed upon the ground and the dogs licked it up. God saw the blood of Naboth. He was very angry with the wicked Jezebel, who had ordered him to be killed and God was angry with Ahab too, because he had allowed Jezebel to write letters.

The judges who had killed Naboth sent to Jezebel, saying, "Naboth is stoned and is dead."

Then Jezebel said to Ahab, "Go and take the vineyard of Naboth; for he is not alive, but dead."

Then Ahab went to the town where the vineyard was, to take it for his own and to make it into a garden.

Do you think that God will punish Ahab for all this wickedness?

God spoke to Elijah and told him what Ahab had done and God said, "Go to the vineyard where Ahab is and tell him that dogs shall one day lick his blood."[1]

So Elijah went to the vineyard. When Ahab saw him he was very sorry; for he could not bear to see Elijah, because he told him of his sins and Ahab said to Elijah, "Have you found me, my enemy?"

He called Elijah his enemy. Then Elijah told him that God had said that dogs should lick his blood and that dogs should one day eat up Jezebel's body and that his children should be eaten by dogs and picked by birds after they were dead.

What a dreadful message this was! I am glad to tell you that Ahab was frightened at the message and was very unhappy. If Ahab had not cared for what God had said, God would have been still more angry with him; but now God soon told Elijah to tell Ahab that He would not give him all the punishment, so that his children should not be killed till after Ahab was dead; they would be eaten by dogs and birds some day, but not for a long while; yet dogs should lick up Ahab's blood.

It was very kind of God not to kill Ahab's children

immediately; but God is very kind even to wicked people, though He casts them into hell at last.

Ahab was still wicked; he was not sorry because he had offended God, for he did not love God; he was only sorry for the punishment. He was not like Saul; he was not like David.

Questions for Chapter 41

What is a garden of grapes called?
Whose vineyard did Ahab want to buy?
When Naboth would not sell it, how did Ahab behave?
How did Jezebel get the vineyard for Ahab?
Who met Ahab in the vineyard?
Why did Ahab call Elijah his enemy?
What did God say should happen at last to Ahab and to Jezebel and to Ahab's children?
Why did God say that Ahab should not have all the punishment?

Scripture Verse

God hates the things that lead to injustice.

'...An heart that deviseth wicked imaginations....A false witness that speaketh lies, ...' - (Prov. 6:16-19).

Notes for Chapter 41

1. The blood of Ahab himself was not licked up by dogs in *that place*, but in Samaria; but the blood of his *son* Joram was licked up in that very place (2 Kings 9:21) and this circumstance was no doubt a fulfilment of God's threatening; but not being sufficiently *direct* for children to understand, it was judged better that this particular of the history should be omitted in this recital.

CHAPTER 42
ELIJAH AND THE DEATH OF THE KING AND QUEEN

1 Kings 22:34-36. 2 Kings 9:30 to end.

I will now tell you how Ahab was killed at last.

A long while afterwards, Ahab went to fight a battle against some people who lived near Canaan. Ahab went to the battle in a chariot drawn by horses. There was a man there who shot an arrow that went into the body of King Ahab and the blood began to run out. The driver of the chariot took Ahab back to the land of Canaan and, as Ahab was on the way home, he died in the chariot. So the chariot was brought back to Ahab's home, full of blood and with Ahab's dead body in it. The servants took the chariot to a pond to wash it and the dogs licked up Ahab's blood.

You remember that God had told Elijah that dogs should lick up Ahab's blood, because Ahab had allowed Naboth to be killed.

All that God says must come true.

Ahab's body was buried in a grave; but his soul, I fear, went to hell; for he did not love God.

And what became of wicked Jezebel!

A long time afterwards she was killed too. A captain ordered her servants to throw her out of the window and they did so and her blood ran out upon the wall and upon the horses of the captain and his soldiers and the captain trampled upon her with his horses' feet. Then he went in to dinner and while he was at dinner, the dogs ate up Jezebel; so that there was nothing left of her but the bone of her head (which is called the skull) and the bones of her feet and hands. This was the end of that wicked woman, who had killed so many of God's good prophets and encouraged Ahab to be wicked.

What dreadful punishments God often sends to wicked people at last!

Now, will you tell me what Ahab should have done, when Naboth said he would not sell his vineyard? Should he have gone on wishing for it and fretting about it? No, that was very wicked; it was coveting. God had said, "You shall not covet." We should not wish for things that God does not choose us to have. If you see something pretty to wear in a shop and you do not have enough money to buy it, you should not go on wishing for it. If your mother puts some cake in the cupboard, you ought not to think to yourself, "I wish I could have some of that cake!" For if you do so, perhaps you will try and take some. (Satan wishes you to wrongly desire after things. How should you stop yourself wishing for things? You should pray to God to take the thoughts out of your mind and to make you think of heavenly things.) Instead of thinking so much of cake and toys and pretty clothes, God's Spirit will help you think, "How good it will be to see the angels and to sing God's praises and to see the dear Lord Jesus on His throne of glory!"

Questions for Chapter 42

How was Ahab killed at last?
Where did he die?
Where did the dogs lick his blood?
Was his body buried?
How was Jezebel killed?
What became of her body?
What is it to covet?
Can we keep ourselves from "coveting"?
What must we do when we begin to covet anything?
What first led Ahab to commit murder?

Scripture Verse

Do not chase after worldly gain.

'...lay up for yourselves treasures in heaven, where neither moth nor rust doth corrupt and where thieves do not break through nor steal: For where your treasure is, there will your heart be also.' - (Matt. 6:20,21).

* * * * * * * * * *

CHAPTER 43
ELIJAH AND THE THREE CAPTAINS

2 Kings 1.

When Ahab was dead, there was another king. He was one of Ahab's sons and his name was A-ha-ziah. He was wicked like his father Ahab and his mother Jezebel. He worshipped idols.

After he had been king a little while, he met with a frightful accident. He was in a room upstairs and he fell out of the window and hurt himself very much. He thought that perhaps he would die and he wanted very much to know whether he would die, or whether he should get well. When you are sick who is it knows whether you shall get well? Only God. But Ahaziah was so foolish that he thought that an idol could tell whether he should die or live. So he sent his servants a great way off to an idol that he had heard of.

As the servants were going to the idol they met a man; they did not know who he was. This man was dressed in the skins of beasts with the hair outside and he wore round his waist a piece of leather, called a girdle. Do you know who this man was? It was Elijah. God had told him to go and speak to the servants of King Ahaziah.

Elijah told the servants that God was angry with Ahaziah

for sending to an idol to know whether he would get well and that God had said that he should never come down from his bed, but should surely die.

How surprised the servants must have been when they found that the man they met knew where they were going and what the king's message was! They did not go on to the idol's house, but they went back to tell Ahaziah what the prophet had said. Then Ahaziah thought that perhaps the prophet was Elijah, for Ahaziah had often heard of him and perhaps Ahaziah had seen him. He said to the servants, "What sort of a man was he?"

And the servants said, "He wore clothes covered with hair and a leather girdle." Then Ahaziah said, "It is Elijah."

Ahaziah was very angry with Elijah for having said that he should die and he wanted to see him; but he knew that Elijah could do wonders, so he determined to send a great many men to fetch Elijah and to make him come. So he ordered a man who could fight, a captain, to take fifty soldiers with him and to go and fetch Elijah.

The captain found Elijah sitting on the top of a hill and the captain spoke to him in a rude manner and said, "You man of God. The king has said, "Come down.""

Elijah said, "If I am a man of God, then let fire come down from heaven and burn up you and your fifty men."

And the fire came down from heaven and burned up the captain and his fifty men.

How dreadful it must have been to have seen all these men burnt up in a moment! How easily God can punish wicked people when He chooses! He might have burnt us up if He had chosen it, but He has been very kind to us.

Ahaziah found that the captain and the soldiers did not come back. Then Ahaziah sent another captain with fifty soldiers and this captain found Elijah on the top of the hill and he said,

"Oh, man of God, the king has said, 'Come down quickly." You see that this captain spoke even more rudely than the other captain had done, for he said, "Come down quickly."

And Elijah answered, "If I am a man of God, let fire come down from heaven and burn you up and your fifty men." And the fire of God came down from heaven and burnt them up. So these soldiers never returned to king Ahaziah

Then he sent another captain and fifty other soldiers. Now this captain had heard what had happened to the other captains.

Do you not think that he must have been very frightened when Ahaziah told him to go and fetch Elijah? What could this poor captain do? The king would have been very angry if he had said he would not go. This is what the captain did. He went to Elijah and he behaved in a very humble manner. He threw himself down upon his knees before Elijah and begged Elijah to spare his life and the lives of his soldiers and not to let them be burnt up like the other soldiers. Was this captain burnt up? Oh, no! God was too kind to burn him up. The angel of the Lord said to Elijah, "Go down with him; don't be afraid of him."

So Elijah went with his captain to King Ahaziah.

Elijah found Ahaziah lying sick in bed and Elijah told him that because he had sent to ask the idol whether he should get well, God would never let him get well, but that he should die in that bed.

Very soon afterwards King Ahaziah died and there was another king instead of him and he was wicked like Ahab and Ahaziah.

Are you not surprised that Ahaziah did not order his servants to kill Elijah? I suppose that he was afraid of hurting Elijah; for God, you see, took care of him. You must pray to God to spare you and He will hear you, because Christ died for you.

Questions for Chapter 43

Who was king when Ahab was dead?
How did he hurt himself?
What did he instruct his servants to ask of a faraway idol?
Whom did the servants meet?
How did he know where the servants were going?
Did the servants know Elijah when they met him?
How did Ahaziah find out that the man whom his servants had met was Elijah?
Why did God burn up the two captains and their fifty soldiers who were sent to Elijah?
Why did God not burn up the third captain?
How may we escape being burnt in hell?

Scripture Verse

God in His love for us has provided a way to be saved.
'For God so loved the world, that he gave his only begotten Son, that whosoever believeth in him should not perish, but have everlasting life.' - (John 3:16).

* * * * * * * * * *

CHAPTER 44
ELIJAH AND THE CHARIOT OF FIRE

2 Kings 2:1-15.

Do you remember that Elijah once wished to die? But God chose that Elijah should never die, but should go up to heaven without dying. How pleased Elijah must have been, when he knew that God meant to do this! Should not you like to be caught up into heaven to see God and to sing with the angels? But God chooses that we should die and that our bodies should be put in the ground. Yet if Christ were to come again while we were alive, then we should be caught up into heaven without dying, if we loved Jesus; but perhaps Jesus may not come for a long while. When Elijah knew that he was soon going up into heaven, he went to a great many places first, where his friends lived. These friends were some good young prophets who lived together and learned about God.

Once Elijah had no friends; he had thought that no one loved God but himself; but now he had a great many friends. These young prophets knew that Elijah was soon going up to heaven. I think they must have felt sorry to part with him; only they knew that he was going to be happy.

Elisha wished very much to see Elijah go up to heaven. What do you think he determined to do?

To keep close to Elijah and not to leave him. Elijah said to him, "Pray stay at this place, while I go to another place, where the Lord has told me to go."

And Elisha said, "I will not leave you."

Soon afterwards Elijah said, "Stay at this place while I go on."

"No," said Elisha, "I will not leave you."

Soon again Elijah said, "Stay at this place while I go on."

"No," said Elisha, "I will not leave you."

So Elijah and Elisha walked a great way together from place to place. At last they came to the river Jordan. Then Elijah took off his cloak and folded it up and struck the waters with it and God made a path through the waters and Elijah and Elisha walked through the river on dry ground.

After they had gone over the river, Elijah said to Elisha, "Ask what I shall do for you before I am taken away from you."

For what did Elisha ask? He wished to be such a prophet

as Elijah was, so he asked for a great deal of his spirit.[1] Was not this a good thing to ask for? Elisha wished to be a great prophet, that he might teach people about God. He did not want people to praise him; he wanted them to praise God.

Elijah said, "You have asked a hard thing, but if you see me when I am taken from you, it shall be so; but if not, it shall not be so."

How much Elisha now hoped that he should see Elijah go up to heaven!

They still walked on and talked to each other. What do you think they talked about? I am sure that they did not talk of foolish things. I think they talked of God and of heaven and of what they could do to please God. How happy Elijah must have felt when he knew he was soon going to see the God he loved so much!

As they were talking, there came down from heaven a chariot and horses of fire, that is, angels, who are bright like the fire and Elijah was taken away from Elisha and carried up into heaven and Elisha saw him go up and he cried out, "My father, my father!"

Elisha loved Elijah as if he had been his father; for he had taught him about God. Elisha was very sorry to lose his dear friend. As Elijah was taken away his cloak fell from him and Elisha picked it up and when Elisha came back to the river Jordan he struck the water with it, as Elijah had done and the waters went up on each side and there was a dry path and Elisha walked over alone.

Now Elisha saw that God had made him such a prophet as Elijah had been. Some of Elijah's friends were standing on the other side of the river and they saw the wonder that Elisha had done and they said, "The spirit of Elijah is in Elisha" and they came and bowed themselves down to him. These young prophets used to listen to what Elijah said and now they wished to listen to Elisha.

Now Elisha would go about from place to place, as Elijah had once done and he would teach people about God and do wonders, to show people that his God was the true God.

You see how happy God made Elijah at last. Once Elijah had been obliged to hide himself, because wicked people had tried to kill him and he had often felt unhappy, because people would not turn to God. At last his tears were wiped away and he went in a bright chariot to heaven. I wish you would begin now to pray to God and think of Him. How happy you would be at last!

Questions for Chapter 44

Why would not Elisha leave Elijah when he told him to stay at several places?
When Elijah allowed Elisha to choose what he would have, what did Elisha choose?
Why did Elisha wish to be a great prophet?
What did Elijah say should be the sign to show Elisha whether he would have what he asked for?
How did Elijah go up to heaven?
What miracle did Elisha do immediately after Elijah had gone?

Scripture Verse

Trust in the Lord as Elijah and Elisha.
'He that dwelleth in the secret place of the most High shall abide under the shadow of the Almighty. I will say of the Lord, He is my refuge and my fortress: my God; in him will I trust.' - (Ps. 91:1,2).

Notes for Chapter 44

1. It is doubtful whether with the words 'a double portion of thy spirit,' Elisha meant double the measure that Elijah had, or double the measure that was bestowed upon the other prophets of his day.

* * * * * * * * * *

CHAPTER 45
ELISHA AND THE BEARS

2 Kings 2:23-25; 4:1-7.

Do you think that people loved Elisha? People who loved God loved Elisha very much, but wicked people hated him. There were some people who even laughed at him; there were even some little children who mocked him. I will tell you about these children.

Did you know that people who have no hair (or only a little hair) on their heads are called bald? Elisha was bald. One day Elisha came near a town where a great many people lived who worshipped idols. One of the golden calves that Jeroboam made was in this town. A great many little children came out of it and met Elisha as he was in the road and they mocked him and said, "Go up, bald head! Go up, bald head!" They wanted Elisha to go up into heaven as Elijah had done, that they might not see him any more, or hear what he said.

How did they dare to speak in this way to the prophet of the Lord? But yet some children dare to take God's name in vain. Elisha turned back and looked on them and told them that God would send them a dreadful punishment.

The children soon found that Elisha had spoken the truth; for two bears came out of the wood and tore forty-two of these children into pieces.

No doubt the children cried and screamed and tried to run away when they saw the bears coming; but it was of no use;

they could not escape; the bears overtook them and killed them. What must their parents have said when they heard what happened to their children? You know how your mother would cry if you were to be eaten up by a bear; but there are no bears or lions in this country. I hope that you will never laugh at people who love God.

You have heard now what became of wicked children who mocked Elisha and you shall hear next of God's kindness to a good poor woman.

This woman had lost her husband, so she was a widow. Her husband had been a good prophet and he had been very poor and he had not been able to pay for all the things he had bought. People should never get into debt, except when they don't have enough money to buy bread; but perhaps this poor prophet did not have enough money to buy bread.

The poor woman came to Elisha and said, "My husband is dead and he did fear the Lord; but I cannot pay my debts and a man is coming to take away my two sons to be slaves."

The poor woman was very unhappy at the thought of losing her dear boys. Your mother would not like you to be taken from her and made a slave. But people in this country may not take away children from their parents; there are no slaves here.

Elisha was sorry for this poor woman and he said, "What shall I do for you? Tell me, what do you have in the house?"

And the woman said, "I have nothing but one pot of oil." This oil was sweet oil and fit to drink.

Elisha said, "Go and borrow a great many empty cups, jugs and basins and bring them into my house. Then shut the door and pour the oil into all these cups and basins and when they are full of oil put them by."

Could a little oil fill a great number of cups and basins? But the woman knew that Elisha could do miracles because God was with him. So the woman did as Elisha had told her. She borrowed the cups, jugs, mugs and basins and shut herself up in a house with her sons and began to pour out the oil. She poured and poured and still there was oil left in her pot. At last she said to her son, "Bring me another cup"; but he said, "There are no more," and then she saw there was no more oil in her pot. So she went to Elisha and asked him what she was to do and he said, "Go and sell your oil and pay your debt and when the debt is paid, keep all the money that is over to buy bread for yourself and your children."

How happy the poor woman must have been! How happy the boys must have been! They were going to be made slaves, but now they might stay with their mother. I hope they grew up to be good like their dead father.

But how sad it is to think of the children who were eaten up by the bears! Perhaps their parents had not taught them to love God. But I do teach you about God. Never laugh at any person who is lame, or blind, or whose back is broken; but more than all, never laugh at people who pray to God. Never laugh at any person who preaches, either in a church or in the streets.

Questions for Chapter 45

What did some wicked children once say to Elisha?
Why did they wish him to go up?
Was Elisha in a temper when he told them that God would punish them?
How many children were eaten up?
What was going to be done to a poor widow, who could not pay her debts?
What was it Elisha ordered her to do?
How long was there oil in the pot?
What did the widow do with the oil?

Scripture Verse

It is important for parents to teach their children the ways of God.

'And ye shall teach them your children, speaking of them when thou sittest in thine house and when thou walkest by the way, when thou liest down and when thou risest up.' - (Deu. 11:19).

* * * * * * * * * *

CHAPTER 46
ELISHA AND THE LITTLE ROOM

2 Kings 4:8-37.

Elisha used to go about from place to place to teach people about God. Those people who loved God were kind to Elisha and gave him food.

There was one very rich lady who used to ask Elisha, whenever he passed by her house, to come in.

This kind woman wished that she had a room in her house for Elisha to sleep in and she said to her husband,[1] "Let us make ready a little room close to our house and let us put in it a bed, a table, a stool and a candlestick, that Elisha may sleep in it when he comes this way."

And the lady's husband allowed her to have such a little room for the prophet. Soon afterwards Elisha came by that way and he slept in this room. Elisha must have liked it very much - he could sit there alone and think of God and he could write in it because there was a table in it and when it was dark he could light the candle and go on writing or reading. I know that he prayed to God in this room; for Elisha often prayed to his God. I hope that you pray in the room you sleep in.

Elisha thought that the woman had been very kind to make such a nice room for him and he wished to do something to please her; for Elisha was grateful; he was very kind to people who were kind to him. Now Elisha had a servant called Gehazi. Elisha instructed Gehazi to ask the woman to come to him. And she came and stood before Elisha. Then Elisha thanked her for her kindness in making the room for him and he asked whether she would like him to speak to the king about her, so that the king might send for her and take notice of her.

Then the woman said, No, she would rather stay where she was and then she went out of the room.

So Elisha said Gehazi, "What shall I do for her?"

And Gehazi said, "She has no child."

Gehazi thought that she would like to have a little child. It was true that this lady and her husband did wish for a child. Then Elisha told Gehazi to call her again and she came and stood at the door.

And Elisha said to her, "Next year you shall have a son."

The woman was very surprised to hear this and she could hardly believe it. Next year she had a baby. She was very fond of him indeed. She thought it was very kind of God to give him to her. Do you not think she loved Elisha more than ever, since he had asked God to give her this child?

One day when the child had grown old enough to talk, he went out with his father into a field where men were reaping corn; for his father had a great many fields full of corn, which his servants reaped. It was the morning, yet the sun was getting hot, for the child soon cried out, "My head, my head!" The child felt such pain in his head that he could not stay in the field.

So the father said to one of his servants, "Carry him to his mother." The servant carried him home to his mother and he sat on her knee till twelve o'clock and then he died.

Oh, how sad the mother was when she found her little boy was dead! I have often heard of little children dying quite suddenly like this poor little boy. Every day we should think, "Am I ready to die if I were to die today?"

Now you shall hear what the mother did with the dead child. She went into the room she had made for Elisha and laid him on his bed and shut the door and went out. Elisha lived at a place a good way off and the lady wished very much to go and see him. I need not tell you why she wished to see him. She asked her husband to allow her to have one of the servants to go with her and one of the donkeys for her to ride upon, that she might go to Elisha and come again soon. And her husband said, "Why do you want to go to Elisha today? This is not the Sabbath day" - because Elisha used to teach people about God on the Sabbath day.

And the woman said, "It shall be well"; but she did not tell her husband why she wanted to go; I suppose she was afraid of grieving him. A servant went with the lady and she said to the servant, "Go quickly and do not stop unless I tell you."

At last they came to the hill where Elisha was. He was with his servant Gehazi. He saw the woman coming while she was still a long way off and he wanted to know why she was coming to him so quickly, for he thought that something was the matter; so he said to Gehazi, "Run now to meet her and say, 'Are things well with you? Are things well with your husband? Are things well with the child?"

So Gehazi ran and asked the woman whether it was well with them. And she said, "It is well." Why did she say it was well? Was not her child dead? But she knew that it was well, or right, because God had made her child die and she knew that all that God does is well. Yet the poor lady felt very unhappy. When she came up to Elisha she got off her donkey and threw her arms round Elisha's feet and Gehazi was going to thrust her away. Was that not very unkind? But Elisha would not let him do so, but said, "Leave her alone; she is very unhappy and God has not told me what has happened to her"; because Elisha only knew those things that God had told him.

Then the woman said to Elisha, "Did I ask you for a son?"

Then Elisha saw that her son was dead. So Elisha gave his own staff, or stick, to Gehazi and told him to go quickly and not to stop to speak to anyone by the way and to lay the staff on the face of the child. But the woman would not go with Gehazi; she said to Elisha; "I will not leave you." She liked better being with Elisha than with unkind Gehazi. She knew that Elisha loved God; Gehazi did not love God; he was wicked, but I am not sure whether the woman knew that he was wicked, for he pretended to be good.

Gehazi went on first and laid the staff on the child's face; but the child did not hear his voice, nor did the child speak; he remained quite dead. So Gehazi went back and met Elisha coming along with the woman and Gehazi said, "The child has not woken up."

At last Elisha came to the house. He went into his own little room and found the child lying dead on the bed. He shut the door and he stayed in the room alone with the dead child. Then he prayed to God to make him alive again and then he lay upon the child, putting his mouth upon the child's mouth and his eyes upon the child's eyes and his hands upon the child's hands and he stretched himself upon him and the child's flesh began to grow warm. Then he got up and walked up and down and then he stretched himself again over the child and the child sneezed seven times and the child opened his eyes.

Then Elisha called Gehazi and instructed him to tell the woman to come. And when she had come into the room Elisha said, "Take up your son," for the child was lying on the bed. Oh how glad the mother was! How thankful to God and to Elisha! Before she took up the child she fell at Elisha's feet and bowed herself to the ground and then she took up her child and went out of the room. Was not this a great wonder that Elisha had done?

Elijah once made a widow's child alive again and Elisha made a child alive again; for Elisha was such a prophet as Elijah had been and could do wonders like him. God had promised that he should be like Elijah, if he saw him taken up to heaven and God kept His promise.

The people of Israel should have minded all that Elisha said, when they heard of the wonders that he did. They might be quite sure that Elisha was a true prophet.

Does God now make little children alive when they die? No, He waits till the last day; then the trumpet shall sound and all the children's bodies shall rise from their graves and the bodies of holy children shall be taken up to heaven, but the bodies of wicked children shall be burned in hell.

Questions for Chapter 46

What did a kind lady build for Elisha?
What did Elisha ask God to give her?
Why was the child sent home to his mother?
Why did the mother go to Elisha when the child was dead?
What was the name of Elisha's servant?
Did Elisha know that the child was dead?
Did prophets know *every* thing that happened?
What things did they know?
Who tried first to make the child alive?
What did Elisha do, when he wished to make the child alive?
If you were to die today, when would your body be raised?

Scripture Verse

Children are special to the Lord.

'But Jesus said, Suffer little children and forbid them not, to come unto me: for of such is the kingdom of heaven.' - (Matt 19:14).

Notes for Chapter 46

1. It is probable this room was already built and that it was over the gateway and separate from the house.

* * * * * * * * * *

CHAPTER 47
ELISHA AND THE LITTLE MAID

2 Kings 5.

There were a great many heathen people, who lived outside the land of Canaan. You know that people who worship idols are called "heathen." Some of these heathen people used often to come into Canaan and rob them and hurt them. Why did God let the people of Israel be robbed and hurt? Because they did not obey Him, or listen to what Elisha had taught them.

Once some of these heathen people came and took away a little girl out of the land of Israel and they sold her as a slave to wait on a rich lady, in a country a great way off. The lady's husband was called Naaman and he was a great captain and could fight well in battle.

But Naaman was very unhappy, for he had a very dreadful disease, called leprosy. He had very sore white places on his body. He could not find anybody who could cure him of his disease. No doctor could cure him; nor could any of the prophets of his idol save him. Now the little girl who waited on his wife had heard of the wonders that Elisha did and she felt sure that he could cure her master and she said, "Oh, that my master were with the prophet that is in my country, for he could cure his leprosy!" Do you think that Elisha could cure Naaman? Yes; God often helped Elisha to do wonders.

Somebody heard what the little girl said and went and told Naaman. Naaman wished very much to be made well and so he determined to go to the land of Israel and to ask Elisha to make him well.

Now Elisha heard that he was coming and Elisha knew that God would help him to make Naaman well and he hoped that when Naaman was made well he would worship the true God, who could do such wonders: for Elisha did not wish people to praise him; he wished them to praise God.

Naaman came into Canaan in a chariot with fine horses and he brought a great many servants with him. Naaman was very proud and he expected that Elisha would pay him a great deal of respect because he was so rich and great. He drove up to Elisha's door; but Elisha did not come out to meet him; he only sent a messenger, who said to Naaman, "Go and wash in the river Jordan seven times and your flesh shall be well."

Then Naaman was very angry and he said, "I thought that the prophet would have come out to me and would have stood and called on the name of the Lord his God and struck his hand over the sore place and made me well." Besides being angry at this, Naaman did not like to wash in a river of the land of Canaan; he would rather have washed in one of the fine large rivers of his own country. Naaman was so very angry, that he was going home to his own country without washing in Jordan; but his servants came to him to persuade him to wash in Jordan. They said, "If the prophet had instructed you to do some very hard thing, would you not have done it, that you might have been made well? Now he tells you to do a very easy thing, only to wash in the river Jordan and will you not do it?" It was kind of the servants to try and persuade Naaman to wash in Jordan.

Naaman listened to what they said, he went to Jordan and he dipped in it seven times and his flesh grew as soft and smooth as the flesh of a little child.

Now Naaman was very glad that he had done as Elisha had told him. I hope he was sorry for having been in such a temper at first.

Where do you think Naaman went when he was well? Did he go home immediately to his own country again? Oh no, that would have been very ungrateful. He went first to Elisha's house and he brought all his servants with him.

He did not feel so proud as he had done before; he did not expect Elisha to come out to him, but he went in to Elisha. He told him that he was sure Elisha's God was the true God and he promised that he would never worship idols any more. How glad Elisha must have been to hear Naaman say that he would worship the true God!

Naaman wished to give Elisha some money and some beautiful things, as a reward for having made him well; so he begged him to take some of the things he had brought with him. But Elisha would not take anything. Why would not Elisha take anything? He wished to show Naaman that he had not made him well that he might get money. You know that Elisha had made him well that he might believe in the true God.

Naaman begged Elisha very much to take something; but Elisha still said he would take nothing. You see that Elisha did not care for money.

Then Naaman set out in his chariot to go back to his own country.

You remember that Elisha had a servant called Gehazi. Gehazi heard his master Elisha say he would not take anything from Naaman and Gehazi wished very much that he could get some of the beautiful things himself; so he thought of a way of getting them by telling lies.

So Gehazi ran after Naaman's chariot; at last Naaman saw him running and he stopped the chariot and got out, for he was afraid that something was the matter. Naaman said, "Is all well?" And Gehazi said, "All is well, but there are two visitors, very good men, who are very poor and my master wants some silver and two suits of clothes to give to them."

Was this true? Naaman did not know that Gehazi was telling lies; so he gave Gehazi twice as much silver as he asked for and put it in two bags and he gave him two suits of clothes and he instructed two of his servants to carry them for Gehazi and Gehazi led the servants to a place with thick walls, where he used to keep things and he instructed the servants to put them there. Then the servants went back to Naaman, to go with him to their own land.

Then Gehazi went to Elisha's house to wait upon Elisha. He little thought that Elisha knew of his wickedness. He thought that Elisha could never find him out, because Naaman was gone a great way and could not tell Elisha that he had given some things to Gehazi. But there was One who saw him. God saw him and God told Elisha what Gehazi had done. And God told Elisha what Gehazi meant to buy with the money. What did Gehazi mean to buy with it?

He meant to buy vineyards and fields and sheep and oxen and slaves. Did Gehazi think that these things could make him happy, while God was angry with him?

Now I will tell you what Elisha said to Gehazi when Elisha saw him.

He said to him, "Where do you come from, Gehazi?" And Gehazi said, "I have not been anywhere." Was that true? You see that Gehazi told another lie to hide his wickedness. Then

Elisha said, "Did not my heart go with you, when Naaman turned again from his chariot to meet you? Let the leprosy of Naaman be upon you forever." Immediately sore white places came on Gehazi's skin and he went out of Elisha's sight. Gehazi could not live with Elisha any more, for people who had leprosy were obliged to live by themselves. I do not know whether he ever repented of his wickedness.

You see how angry God is with liars and what dreadful punishments He sends them. Never try to get things by telling lies, for even if no one should find you out, God sees you. Perhaps you have told lies already. Confess your lies to God. He will forgive you, because Jesus died that sinners might be forgiven.

Questions for Chapter 47

What are people called who worship idols?
What did the heathen people who lived near Canaan sometimes do to the people of Israel?
Who was Naaman?
What dreadful disease was upon Naaman?
How did he hear of Elisha?
How did Naaman expect Elisha to behave to him?
Why didn't Naaman like to bathe in the Jordan?
Why did Naaman, when he was cured, think that Elisha's God was the true God?
What did Naaman determine never to do again?
Why didn't Elisha take any presents from Naaman?
Who coveted Naaman's presents?
What did Gehazi say in order to get the presents?
How did Elisha know what Gehazi had done?
What lie did Gehazi tell Elisha?
What punishment did God give to Gehazi?

Scripture Verse

God hates Lies.

'These six things doth the Lord hate: yea, seven are an abomination unto him: A proud look, a lying tongue and hands that shed innocent blood, An heart that deviseth wicked imaginations, feet that be swift in running to mischief, A false witness that speaketh lies and he that soweth discord among brethren.' - (Prov. 6:16-19).

* * * * * * * * * *

CHAPTER 48
THE LAST KING OF ISRAEL, AND HIS PEOPLE

2 Kings 17:1-24.

I have told you a great deal about Elisha. You have heard what a great many wonders he did. Did the people of Israel listen to what he said or did they still go on in wickedness? They went on in their wickedness.

At last Elisha died. God did not take him up to heaven in a chariot of fire. He died in his bed and his spirit went to heaven, but his body was buried in the ground. After Elisha was dead, the people of Israel grew still more wicked. King Ahab had been a very wicked king and Ahaziah his son had been wicked and the king was wicked and when he died, there was another king and he was wicked and at last he died and there was another king and he was wicked and there were a great many kings of Israel, one after the other and they were all wicked. At last God determined to send a great punishment to all the people of Israel. You shall hear what it was.

There was a king who lived far away, in a country called Assyria. He was very rich but worshipped idols not God and he had a great many soldiers who could fight well. The king of Assyria came with his soldiers into the land of Canaan and fought against the people and conquered them. He got into all their towns and took away the things in them and took the people away to be their slaves. How unhappy the people of Israel were when they were taken away from their houses and gardens and obliged to go a great way off and work very hard!

This was thc punishment God sent them at last, because they would worship idols and do many wicked things. They never came into their own country again, but heathen people came and lived in it.

I hope that you will not be like the people of Israel; that you will worship only God, not idols. Punishment eventually comes to those who turn from God.

Questions for Chapter 48

Did the people of Israel listen to what Elisha said and leave off doing wicked things?
Was Elisha taken up to heaven without dying?
Which king came at last to fight against the people of Israel?
What did the King of Assyria do with the people of Israel when he had conquered them?
Why did God let them be taken away from their own land?

Scripture Verse

The people of God suffered for worshipping idols rather than Him.

'And they served their idols: which were a snare unto them.' - (Ps. 106:36)

CHAPTER 49
HEZEKIAH AND THE KING WHO TRUSTED IN GOD

2 Kings 18; 19.

I am now going to speak to you about something I told you a long while ago. I shall be very pleased if I find that you have not forgotten it, for it is a thing hard to remember. Do you remember that God had been angry with King Solomon and that God had said his son should be king over only part of Canaan? What God had said came true. Jeroboam took away a great deal of the land from Solomon's son. Jeroboam was called the king of Israel and Solomon's son was called the king of Judah. Now Solomon's son lived in Jerusalem, but Jeroboam lived in the other part of the land.

I have told you about some of the kings of Israel, about Ahab and Ahaziah, but there were a great many more besides and they were all wicked, so that God let the king of Assyria come at last and take the king and the people of Israel into Assyria, which was a country a great way off.

I have not told you about the kings of Judah. When Solomon's son died, his son was king of Judah and when he died his son was king, so there were a great many kings one after another; some of the kings of Judah were good and some were wicked. At last there was a good king, called Hez-e-ki-ah.

He lived at Jerusalem and he liked to worship God in the temple and he persuaded a great many people to come and worship God; for Hezekiah loved God. Now you shall hear what care God took of Hezekiah. God had let the king of Assyria take away the people of Israel. Would God let him hurt the good king of Judah? Hear what God did.

The king of Assyria sent some of his soldiers to Jerusalem and they brought their tents and waited all round the city and tried to get in. The people shut the gates fast; still they were afraid in case the king of Assyria's soldiers should get in at last. But Hezekiah knew that God could keep them from being hurt. The people of Assyria spoke very wicked words against God, while they were waiting outside Jerusalem and one day the king of Assyria wrote a letter and sent it to Hezekiah.

It was a very wicked letter; this was what was written in it. "Your God cannot save you from the king of Assyria, who has conquered a great many countries; the gods of those people could not save them, neither can your God save you."

Some men brought this letter to king Hezekiah and he read it. He could not bear to read such wicked words against God, so he took it into the temple and spread the letter before God and began to pray. He said, "Oh, God, You are the true God; You have made heaven and earth. Other gods are only idols, made of wood and stone; they could not keep people from being hurt. Oh, save us from the king of Assyria, that everybody may know that You are the only God."

God heard Hezekiah's prayer. Now I will tell you what God did that night. He sent His angel to kill a great many of the people of Assyria as they lay in their tents. The angel did not kill them all, but the rest were very frightened when they found that so many had died in the night and they went back to their own country and they did not get into Jerusalem.

So God saved Hezekiah, king of Judah. Hezekiah was glad that all the people saw that his God was the true God. God can keep all people from being hurt. What should we do when we are frightened? We should pray to God to save us.

Does it never frighten you to think of the devil and all his wicked angels? Now is the time to pray to God to save us from them. God will hear us.

Why will He hear us? Is it because we are good that He will hear us? No, that is not the reason; for no one is really good. But this is the reason - because He is kind and good and because He promised Jesus that He would hear us. Jesus died that His Father might hear our prayers and forgive us our sins.

Questions for Chapter 49

What punishment had God given to Solomon a long while before Elisha died?
What was *that* part of the land called which Jeroboam was king over?
What was *that* part of the land called which Solomon's son was king over?
Was Jerusalem in Judah, or in Israel?
What became at last of the people of Israel?
Were there a great many kings, one after the other, over Judah?
Were any of them good?
Who was Hezekiah?
Which king sent soldiers to fight against Jerusalem?
Why did the king of Assyria think that he should be able to conquer Jerusalem?
What did Hezekiah do with the wicked letter that the king of Assyria wrote to him?
How did God save Hezekiah from the king of Assyria?
What should we do when we feel afraid?
Why will God hear our prayers?

Scripture Verse

God in His written Word encourages us to pray to him.
'Be careful for nothing; but in everything by prayer and supplication with thanksgiving let your requests be made known unto God.' - (Phil. 4:6).

CHAPTER 50
THE LAST KING OF JUDAH AND HIS PEOPLE

2 Chron. 36:11-20.

How kind God had been to Hezekiah, king of Judah!

God would not let the people of Assyria hurt him. At last Hezekiah died and there was another king and at last he died and there was another king and at last he died and there was another king and so there were a great many kings, one after another and most of them were very wicked. Most of the people of Jerusalem were wicked and worshipped idols. So God sent prophets to tell them that he would not keep them from being hurt any more and that He would let some heathen king take them a great way off. You remember that the people in the other part of Canaan (who were called the people of Israel) had been taken away by the king of Assyria and God said that the people of Judah should be taken away by some other king.

At last there came a rich proud king, called Nebuchadnezzar, to fight against the people in Jerusalem. This king came from a country called Babylon. He had a great many soldiers, who placed their tents all round Jerusalem. At last they got into the city and they broke down the wall and they burnt a great number of the fine houses. They even burnt the beautiful temple that Solomon had built. They took away the golden things that he had put in it; the gold basins, candlesticks, altars, spoons, cups and treasures and they took them to Babylon, to put them in the house of their idols.

There was a king in Jerusalem named Zedekiah. Nebuchadnezzar took this king and put out both his eyes and brought him to Babylon and kept him in prison, till he died. Nebuchadnezzar killed a great many people and he took a great many more to be slaves with him in Babylon.

How sorry the people were to leave their land and go to Babylon! They sat down by the rivers of Babylon and wept and they would not sing psalms as they used to, but they hung their harps upon the willow trees that grew by the water side.[1]

Why did God let them be taken from the land of Canaan? Because they had sinned against Him by breaking His laws and hurting His prophets. At last He would punish them, as He had said He would.

Questions for Chapter 50

Were there any more kings over Judah, after Hezekiah died?
Why did God at last let the people of Jerusalem be taken away to another country?
Who took them away?
Did he take the king away?
What was his name?
What became of him?
What became of the temple?

Scripture Verse

God forewarned His people that disobedience would bring disaster.

'The Lord shall bring thee and thy king which thou shalt set over thee, unto a nation which neither thou nor thy fathers have known and there shalt thou serve other gods, wood and stone.' - (Deu. 28:36).

Notes for Chapter 50

1. Ps.137.

SECTION 4

DANIEL

Introduction

The book of Daniel is the story of some young Jewish exiles who are determined to follow God's ways, despite the danger. They are called Daniel, Hananiah, Mishael and Azariah but their Babylonian captors rename them Belteshazzar, Shadrach, Meshach and Abednego. The men have been chosen and trained to serve the King of Babylon, but they continue to be obedient to God. When the Babylonians try to kill them for not serving their gods and idols, God steps in to bless and protect them.

Some Suggestions for Study

Do you ever feel like Daniel and his friends? Do you find it hard not to join in with others when they are doing something you know is wrong? Maybe others use bad words and make you feel as if you should. Do you feel you have to wear the same clothes as them or buy the same things? How many things do you do just because others do it? Do you feel that others would make fun of you because you want to obey God? Pray that God will guide you in how to choose how to live. Also pray that God will give you courage to do what is right, even if nobody else does.

CHAPTER 51
DANIEL AND THE GOLDEN IMAGE

Dan. 3.

Some of the people who were taken to Babylon loved God. I will tell you about three young men who loved God very much and who would not worship idols.

Nebuchadnezzar once made a very large image of gold; it was higher than a very tall tree. This image was placed out of doors and Nebuchadnezzar sent for all the judges and captains in his land and for a great many rich people, to come and see this golden image. Now Nebuchadnezzar had made the three good young men judges; so that they were obliged to come and see the golden image. When all these captains and judges and rich men had come, they stood round the image and a man called out very loudly, "Oh, people, when the music begins to play, then fall down and worship the golden image that Nebuchadnezzar has set up. Whoever does not fall down and worship shall immediately be cast into a burning fiery furnace."

Do you know what a furnace is? It is a place full of fire; it is like a very large oven. How horrible it must be to be put into a furnace! Would the three good young men worship the image, or would they not? Very soon the music began to play and the people fell down and worshipped the image.

Then some men came to Nebuchadnezzar and said, "Oh, king, live forever. Did you not instruct that every man should fall down and worship the golden image, when the music was played and that if anyone did not worship, he should be cast into a fiery furnace? There are three men who have not done what you said; they never worship your gods, nor have they worshipped the golden image."

Then Nebuchadnezzar was in a rage and he commanded the men to be brought to him. Then these men were brought before the king. And Nebuchadnezzar said to them, "Is it true that you do not worship my gods, nor the golden image that I have set up? Now if next time the music is played, you fall down and worship, it is well; but if not, you shall be cast into the furnace. And who is the God that deliver you out of my hand?"

Then the young men answered the king, "Oh, Nebuchadnezzar, our God is able to deliver us from the burning fiery furnace and He will deliver us out of your hand, Oh, king. But if not, we will not serve your gods, nor worship the golden image you have set up."

Then Nebuchadnezzar was full of fury and his face looked quite different from before, because he was in such a passion.

He asked his servants to make the furnace seven times hotter than usual and he ordered the strongest of his soldiers to throw the three young men into the furnace. First the young men were bound, so that they might not be able to move when they were in the fire and their clothes were not taken off. Then the strong soldiers threw them into the furnace and the flames were so great that the soldiers caught fire and were burnt up. The three young men fell down in the furnace.

Nebuchadnezzar was near the furnace and watched to see the young men burning. But oh! how surprised he was to see them walking about the furnace and to see a man with them, who looked like the Son of God!

Nebuchadnezzar cried out to his servants, "Did we not throw three men into the fire?" and they answered, "True, Oh, king." And Nebuchadnezzar said, "I see four men loose, walking in the midst of the fire and they are not hurt and one of them is like the Son of God."

Nebuchadnezzar had never seen the Son of God; but he

had never seen a man like him who was in the furnace; so he supposed that he must be a god. Was it not kind of God to come and walk with these young men in the furnace?

Then Nebuchadnezzar went to the furnace and called the three young men by their names and said, "Oh, servants of the Most High God, come out of there." And the three young men came out of the furnace. Then all the judges and captains, came near and looked at the young men and saw that they were not the least hurt, not a hair of their heads was singed, nor were their clothes scorched, nor did they even smell of fire. Then Nebuchadnezzar saw that there was a God who could deliver His servants from the burning flame and Nebuchadnezzar said that if any person spoke against this God he should be cut to pieces and his house should be made a dung-hill. And the king was very pleased with these three young men.

Do you think that the young men had been happy while they were in the fire? Yes, I think they must have been happy, for they had such a friend walking with them. Were they not glad that they had not worshipped the golden image? If they had been burnt, their spirits would have gone to heaven; but God did not let them be burnt, that all people might see that He was the true God and that everybody should worship Him. Though all the other people worshipped the image, they did not. If other people do wicked things, should we do them too?

If all your firends do a naughty thing you should still do what is right, so that you may please God. If you see everybody else breaking the Sabbath day, remember that you ought to keep it. If other children are disobedient and join in doing something they are not allowed to do, still remember God sees you.

Questions for Chapter 51

Did any of the people of Judah who were taken to Babylon love God?
What wicked thing did they refuse to do?
What did the three young men tell Nebuchadnezzar that their God was able to do?
What became of the strong men who put the good young men in to the furnace?
Who walked with them in the fire?
What did Nebuchadnezzar say about the true God when he saw that the young men had not been hurt by the fire?
Why had God done this great wonder?

Scripture Verse

We should desire to be led by God.
'Search me, Oh, God and know my heart: try me and know my thoughts: And see if there be any wicked way in me and lead me in the way everlasting.' - (Ps. 139:23,24).

* * * * * * * * * *

CHAPTER 52
BELSHAZZAR AND THE WRITING ON THE WALL

Dan. 5.

At last Nebuchadnezzar, the proud king of Babylon, died and there was another king of Babylon, called Belshazzar. He was the grandson of Nebudchadezzar and he was like Nebuchadnezzar; for he was proud and he worshipped idols.

One day he made a great feast and a great many rich men, called lords, came to his feast and Belshazzar drank wine before them. Do you remember that Nebuchadnezzar had taken the gold and silver cups that were in the temple at Jerusalem and brought them to Babylon? Belshazzar instructed that these cups might be brought for him and his Lords and his wives to drink wine out of them. So they were brought and Belshazzar and his Lords and his wives, drank wine in them and while they drank, they praised their idols, which were made of gold and silver, of bronze, of iron, of wood and of stone.

Was it not wicked of Belshazzar and his lords, to take the cups which were once in the house of the true God and to praise idols while they were drinking in them?

Oh yes and God was very angry, because Belshazzar had heard about the true God and yet he worshipped idols and praised them. Now you shall hear what God did to Belshazzar.

Did not God see this wickedness?

While he was drinking, the king saw the fingers of a man's hand, writing on the wall of the palace, near where the candlestick was. He did not see a man, only some fingers. The king was very frightened; he did not look merry any longer, but he trembled very much and his knees knocked against each other.

Belshazzar wanted to know what was written on the wall; there were four words written there, but the king could not read that kind of writing, so he sent for all the men in Babylon who were called wise and clever and who said they could tell hard things.

Belshazzar said, "Whoever will read that writing and tell the meaning of it, shall be clothed in scarlet (such as kings used to wear) and shall have a golden chain round his neck and shall be made a great judge."

A great many people tried to read the writing, but they could not. Then Belshazzar was still more frightened and looked very terrified and his lords were also frightened. They were afraid that something very dreadful had been written on the wall; they thought something sad was going to happen. Now Belshazzar had a mother. She was called the Queen. She heard what had happened and she came into the room where Belshazzar was and said, "Oh, king, live forever. Do not be frightened, there is a man in Babylon who is very wise indeed and who can tell the meaning of things; his name is Daniel. Let him be called and he will know the meaning of the writing."

Now this Daniel was one of the men whom Nebuchadnezzar had brought from Jerusalem; he was an Israelite. When he first came to Babylon he was quite young, but now he was old; he was very wise and he loved God very much.

Belshazzar commanded Daniel to come to him. Belshazzar then said, "I hear that you can tell the meaning of things; if you can read the writing on the wall and tell the meaning of it, you shall be clothed in scarlet and wear a gold chain and be made a great judge."

But Daniel said, "I do not want any reward, yet I will read the writing and tell the meaning of it." Then Daniel told Belshazzar that the true God was very angry with him for being so proud and for sending for the cups of his temple and for drinking in them and praising idols and for not worshipping God though he had heard of Him. Daniel said that the writing on the wall meant that he should soon be king no more, but that some people would come and take his land away from him.

Then Belshazzar commanded that Daniel should be clothed in scarlet and wear a golden chain about his neck and that many people should obey him.

That very night a king from another country got into Babylon, with a great many soldiers and killed Belshazzar and took his throne and his crown and all he had. So the words that God had written on the wall came true.

What has God written down in His book about those who do not love Him? Has He not said that He will come and punish them?

Does it frighten you to think of this day? It certainly will come.

I have often told you what we should pray for; so I hope that you are praying for the Holy Spirit.

Questions for Chapter 52

What was the name of the king of Babylon, who made a feast to a great many of his lords?
Which golden cups did Belshazzar and his Lords drink out of?
Whom did they praise while they were drinking?
What did Belshazzar see, which frightened him very much?
How many words were written on the wall?
Whom did Belshazzar send for *at first* to tell him the meaning of the words?
Whom did the queen advise him to send for?
Who was Daniel? Was he a heathen or an Israelite?
What was the meaning of the words on the wall?
What rewards did Belshazzar give Daniel?
How soon did the words come true?
What dreadful thing has God said shall happen that we shall see?

Scripture Verse

God desires to give His Spirit to those who are his children.
'If ye then, being evil, know how to give good gifts unto your children: how much more shall your heavenly Father give the Holy Spirit to them that ask him?' - (Luke 11:13).

CHAPTER 53
DANIEL AND THE DEN OF LIONS

Dan. 6.

The name of the king that conquered Belshazzar was Da-ri-us. He was a proud man and he worshipped idols; yet he liked Daniel very much and he set him over all the other judges and lords and told all the people to listen to him. Daniel was a very wise old man and he was fit to be a judge. There were a great many rich men who hated Daniel, because the king told them to listen to Daniel and because the king liked Daniel better than them. These men were envious of Daniel. They were like Cain, who was envious of Abel and like Joseph's brothers, who were envious of Joseph.

Perhaps you have some times felt envious, when you have heard people praise another child and seen them give him presents. Then you were like Satan. You must pray to God to keep you from being envious, for we are very good at being envious because we have wicked hearts.[1]

These wicked rich men wished to hurt Daniel and to disgrace him to King Darius; but they did not know how to do it. They never saw Daniel do anything wrong. I suppose they were afraid of telling the king lies about Daniel, in case they should be found out. But at last they thought of a way to get Daniel into disgrace. They knew that he prayed very often to his God; so they went to the king and asked him to make a law that no one should pray to any God or man, but to the king himself, for thirty days and that if anyone did pray to anyone else, he should be cast into a den of lions. Now the king did not know why these men asked him to make this law; if the king had known that Daniel always prayed to his God, I do not think he would have made this law, for the king loved Daniel.

The king was foolish to say that he would do as these men wished, because you know, the king was a heathen and he did not love the true God. So he wrote down the law and promised not to change it.

Daniel heard of the law that the king had made. Do you think that he went on praying? Daniel would have thought it very dreadful not to pray to God for thirty days. He wanted to praise God very often and ask Him to bless him.

He used always to pray before the open window in his room. Perhaps you know why he did so. The reason was, he liked to look towards the place where Jerusalem was. He could not see Jerusalem from his window, because he was so far off; but still he knew which way it was and he knew that God loved Jerusalem and that God used to come down into the temple, before it was burnt; so Daniel liked to look that way when he prayed. He knelt down three times every day and prayed and thanked God for all His kindness to him.

The men who hated Daniel heard that he went on praying; so they went one day to look at him praying, that they might tell the king that they had seen him.

Then they asked the king, "Did you not make a law that if anyone prayed to any God or man, excepting you, that he should be cast into a den of lions?" And the king said, "Yes, it is true and I cannot change the law."

Then the men said, "That Daniel, who was brought from Jerusalem to be a slave, does not listen to you, nor your law, but prays three times a day."

Then the king was very sorry that he had made a law against praying and tried to think of some way of not letting Daniel be killed; but he could think of no way. In the evening the men came to him and said, "You cannot alter the law that you have made, for in our country it is a law that laws may not be altered."

Then the king commanded Daniel to be brought and he was cast into a den of lions; the lions lived in a deep place underground. Lions are always very hungry in the evening and roar for their food. Would they not eat up Daniel as soon as he was thrown into the den?

But Darius knew that Daniel's God was a very great God and he said to Daniel, "Your God, whom you serve always, is able to deliver you."

I think Darius must have heard how God once saved three men from being burnt in the furnace. A stone was brought and laid upon the top of the den and the king put his seal on it, that none might take away the stone and he put on it also the seal of the men that hated Daniel.

Why did the king put his own seal on it? That he might find out if anyone came and took Daniel away, for no one else had a seal like the king's; so if any broke the seal the king would find it out. Why did he put the wicked men's seal? That they might see that the king did not take Daniel out in the night.

The king went to his palace that evening, but he was so unhappy that he could not eat and he would not let his servants play music to him as usual and when he went to bed he could not sleep.

He got up very early in the morning. Where did he go? To the den of lions. When he came to the den, he cried out in a very loud voice, "Oh, Daniel, is the God, whom you serve always, able to deliver you from the lions?" The king longed to hear Daniel's voice - and he heard it. Daniel said, "Oh, king, live forever. My God has sent his angel and has shut the lions' mouths, that they have not hurt me, because I had done nothing wrong."

Then the king was very glad indeed and he commanded that Daniel should be taken up and he was not the least hurt.

Why did God take such care of Daniel?

Because Daniel loved Him and feared Him and God wanted to show the king that He was able to save Daniel and that He was the true God.

The king was very angry with those men who had asked him to put Daniel in the den and he commanded them to be thrown down into the den, with their wives and their children. It was very cruel of the king to have the wives and children put into the den, but the wicked men deserved to be put there.[2] The lions ate them up in a moment and broke all their bones before they came to the bottom of the den. So you see that the lions were very hungry - though they did not eat Daniel.

Then King Darius wrote a letter and sent it to all countries and said that he had made a law that everyone should fear the God of Daniel, because He was the true God, who could do wonders and who had saved Daniel from the lions.

Do not you wish that everybody had minded this law and feared the God of Daniel? But they did not; they still went on worshipping idols. You see how much Daniel loved God; he would rather have died than not have prayed to God.

Shall *you* be cast into a den of lions if you pray to God? No you may pray to God without fear. I hope you do pray very often. You should not pray, as Daniel did, before a window. I told you his reason for doing so. You should pray in some quiet place; God can see you in every place and He will hear you if you pray with your heart, whether you are kneeling by your bedside, or in a corner of the room, or in a little room by yourself. He will even hear your prayers when you are walking in the lane, or in the garden.

If you should be sleeping in a room where there are wicked people, who would laugh at you for praying and for reading the Bible - you should still do it. You should always think that God sees you. You should be more afraid of making Him angry than of anything else.

Some children forget to pray in the morning and are too sleepy to pray at night. They pray in a great hurry and without thinking or caring for God. Does God hear such prayers?

Questions for Chapter 53

What was the name of the king who conquered Belshazzar?
What did King Darius say Daniel should be?
Why did some rich men hate Daniel?
What law did they ask Darius to make?
Why did they ask him to make this law?
How often used Daniel to pray every day?
Why did he open his window towards Jerusalem?
Who came one day to look at Daniel when he was praying?
Why did the king not change the law when he heard that Daniel had been praying?
Why did not the king sleep, or eat that night?
Who did Daniel say God had sent to take care of him?
Who were put in the den when Daniel was taken out?
What did King Darius ask all people to do in his letter t?
Of what should you be more afraid than of anything else?

Scripture Verse

Do not worry God tells us to bring our needs to Him in prayer.

'Be careful for nothing; but in everything by prayer and supplication with thanksgiving let your requests be made known unto God.' - (Phil. 4:6).

Notes for Chapter 53

1. James 3:16. 2. Deu. 24:16

SECTION 5

EZRA

Introduction

The book of Ezra is among of the last of the historical books of the Old Testament and it records one of the final episodes in God's plan before the coming of Jesus.

The books of 1 and 2 Kings (and 1 and 2 Chronicles) record that despite God's constant warnings, the Israelites turn to worship the false gods of the surrounding nations and fail to keep His commands. Therefore, God allows the people to be conquered and taken away into exile.

In the book of Ezra (and also Nehemiah) God enables the people to return to the Promised Land and rebuild the temple and Jerusalem. God moves Cyrus, the King of the Persians, to release the people and help them back to their land. Cyrus chooses Ezra, an Israelite teacher of the Law of Moses, to help God's people to follow the Law once again.

Some Suggestions for Study

Think about a place you'd like to call home. How does it feel to return there after being away, perhaps after a holiday or school? Write down or draw the things that you like about home.

God has promised us a home better than we could ever imagine – our heavenly home. Just as we look forward to coming home after being away, pray that God will give us an excitement about going to our new home in heaven.

CHAPTER 54
THE RETURN TO JERUSALEM

Ezra 1; 3; 6:14 to end.

I told you how unhappy the poor Israelites were in Babylon. They wished very much to return to their own country, Canaan, but the king of Babylon would not let them go back. However, God had made a promise, a long while before, that He would let them return some day.[1]

Now, there was another king in Babylon besides Darius, who was a king as well as him. His name was Cyrus. God put it in the heart of Cyrus to let the poor Israelites return to their own country. For God remembered His promise. Cyrus had been taught to worship idols, yet he believed that Daniel's God was the true God and he was ready to obey what the true God said.

So Cyrus told the Israelites they could go back to their own country and build the temple at Jerusalem. Cyrus gave back all the gold and silver that Nebuchadnezzar had taken out of the temple - dishes, basins, cups of gold and silver. Many of the people in Babylon gave the Israelites presents before they went away; horses, camels and donkeys, to carry their things.

How happy the poor Israelites were to leave such a wicked place as Babylon! But oh! When they had come to Jerusalem, how sad to see the walls broken down and many of the houses burnt! But still the Israelites were very thankful to God for letting them come here again.

You remember that God never let the people who had lived in the other part of Canaan come back. It was kind of God to let the people of Judah come back. When they were come to Jerusalem they set up the altar and offered a great many beasts on it, to show how grateful they were.

They wished to build the temple as soon as they could and they got a great many carpenters and masons and they sent for beautiful trees to help to build it.

At last they laid the first stone of the temple upon the high hill in Jerusalem. A great many Israelites all came together to see the first stone laid. The priests stood near dressed in white, with trumpets and the singers played music and sang psalms, saying, "The Lord is good and His mercy endures forever."

And when the first stone was laid, the priests blew the trumpets and the singers sang psalms and the people shouted for joy.

There were some old people there, who remembered having seen the temple before it was burnt, a long while ago, when they were little children and when the other people shouted these old people wept very loud. Why did they weep? Why had the temple been burnt? Because the people had been wicked. Perhaps the old men were grieved because the people had been so ungrateful to God. The noise of weeping and the shouting could be heard a great way off.

The people of Israel were a great many years building the temple. At last it was finished and the people were very glad. This temple was not so beautiful as the temple Solomon had built and God did not come down in a cloud and fill it.

You will be glad to hear that the Israelites determined to worship idols no more. But though they did not worship idols, they did not love God with all their hearts; so they did a great many other wicked things. There were a few of them who really loved God.

The Israelites lived in Jerusalem and in the land of Canaan a great many years. They were now called Jews instead of Israelites. God sent them prophets sometimes, to teach them and to make them remember the promise that He had made to Abraham. What promise do I mean? That a Saviour should one day be born, who should be their King forever. God had made the same promise to David and had said that this Saviour should be one of his children's children's children's children.[2] Some of the Israelites, or Jews, thought very often of this promise and longed for the Saviour to be born into the world.[3] They knew that the Saviour would be born in Bethlehem, where David was born. How did they know that? Because one of the prophets had said that He should be born in Bethlehem,[4] and they knew that His mother would be some person of the family of David, because the prophets had said so and they knew that He would be the King of the Jews and of all people, for the prophets had said so.

At last one of David's great-great-great, etc., grandchildren, a woman called Mary, had a son, who was the Son of God and He was born in Bethlehem.

You have heard about this baby and how the Jews or Israelites crucified Him. You will soon read about Him in the Bible. Do you love this Saviour? His Father sent Him to suffer the punishment of Adam's sins and of my sins and of your sins and of the Jews' sins and of all people's sins.[5] Before the world was made, God told His Son to come and die;[6] and the Son promised that He would come.[7] At last He came and died and one day He will come again. When He comes again, He will bring with Him all those who cared for God's promise and longed for the Saviour to come. Abel will come with Jesus and Noah and Abraham and Isaac and Jacob and Joseph and Moses and Joshua and David and Elijah and Elisha and Hezekiah and Daniel and a great many more. All these men lived *before* Jesus came down to die; but you live *after* Jesus has come. God has kept His promise - Jesus has died for your sins. Do you love the Lord Jesus Christ and His Father? If you do, it is a sign that God has put His Spirit into your hearts.

Then you too will live with Jesus in heaven and you will sit down with Abraham, Isaac and Jacob and Joseph and Moses and David.

Questions for Chapter 54

Who was Cyrus? What kind thing did he do to the Israelites?
Why did God put it into Cyrus's heart to let the Israelites return to their own land?
What did Cyrus give to the Israelites?
What did the Israelites build in Jerusalem?
What sounds were heard when the first stone of the temple was laid?
Did the Israelites go on worshipping idols?
Did they really love God?
What promise did all the prophets speak of?
Where did the prophets say this Saviour would be born?
Of whose family did the prophets say His mother would be?
Did the Saviour come at last? Will He come again?
Whom will He bring with Him?

Scripture Verse

The Bible says that we will receive the final promise with those who have gone before us.
'And these all, having obtained a good report through faith, received not the promise: God having provided some better thing for us, that they without us should not be made perfect.' - (Heb. 11:39,40).

Notes for Chapter 54

1. Jer. 29:10.
2. 1 Chron. 17:11,13; compare with Heb. 1:5.
3. Luke 2:38.
4. Mic. 5:2.
5. Isa. 53:6.
6. 1 Pet. 1:20.
7. John 10:18.

A FEW PRINCIPAL QUESTIONS

FOR CHILDREN
WHO HAVE FINISHED READING THIS BOOK.

1. Why was God displeased with Eli?
2. What did God tell little Samuel in the night?
3. Who took away the ark?
4. Why did the Philistines send it back to Canaan?
5. Was Eli a king or a judge?
6. Who was the king of Israel when Eli was judge?
7. Who was judge after Eli was dead?
8. Why did the Israelites ask for a king?
9. Whom did God choose for their king at first?
10. What disobedient thing did he do?
11. What punishment did God give him?
12. What was David before he was made king?
13. What are David's songs called?

14. Whom did David fight against when all other people were afraid?

15. Why did Saul try to kill David?

16. How did Saul die?

17. Why did God put it into the hearts of the Israelites to make David king?

18. On what mountain did David place the ark? Where was Mount Zion?

19. Why wouldn't God allow David to build a house for the ark?

20. What very wicked thing did David do after he was king?

21. What punishment did God say he should have?

22. Who was king after David?

23. What did Solomon ask God to give him?

24. What sin did he commit in his old age?

25. What punishment did God say he should have?

26. Who was Jeroboam?

27. Why did he teach his people to pray to two golden calves?

28. Who was Ahab?

29. Which idol did he worship?

30. Which prophet did he try to kill?

31. Why did not God send rain for three years?

32. How was Elijah kept alive during that time?

33. Why did God say that dogs should lick up Ahab's blood?

34. Who saw Elijah go up to heaven?

35. What punishment did God give at last to the people of Israel?

36. What was that part of the land called which God let Solomon's son be king over?

37. Which great city was in Judah?

38. What was the other part of the land called?

39. Who was Hezekiah - a king of Judah or a king of Israel?

40. From which king did God deliver him?

41. What punishment did God give to the people of Judah?

42. Why did Nebudchadnezzar once put three young men of Judah in the fire?

43. Who told Belshazzar the meaning of the writing on the wall?

44. What happened to Belshazzar that night?

45. Why did Darius put Daniel in the den of lions?

46. What king allowed the Israelites to go back to Canaan again?

47. After they had gone back what did they build?

48. Who was born in Bethlehem after a long while had passed?

NOTES

NOTES

NOTES

NOTES

NOTES

NOTES

NOTES

NOTES